The White Witch of Rose Hall's SpellBook

The White Witch of Rose Hall's SpellBook

Matthew Petchinsky

The White Witch of Rose Hall's SpellBook
By: Matthew Petchinsky

Disclaimer for *The White Witch of Rose Hall's Spellbook*

This spellbook is a work of both respect and creative inspiration, honoring the legacy and mystique of the legendary White Witch of Rose Hall. The author, a devoted admirer of the stories surrounding her life and her craft, has written this book as an homage to her memory, acknowledging her as a powerful figure in the world of witchcraft and lore. Every effort has been made to approach her legacy with the respect and reverence it deserves.

For Entertainment and Educational Purposes Only

While the spells, rituals, and practices included in *The White Witch of Rose Hall's Spellbook* are based on historical, folkloric, and creative interpretations, they are not guaranteed to produce specific outcomes and should not be taken as definitive instructions for practicing witchcraft or magical arts. This book is intended as a source of inspiration, education, and entertainment. It is not a substitute for professional advice or services, whether they be legal, medical, financial, or otherwise.

Responsibility and Accountability

The spells and practices described in this book are not to be taken lightly. Practicing witchcraft involves intent, focus, and personal responsibility. The energies and forces invoked in these spells can have unpredictable consequences if approached without care, respect, or preparation. The author strongly advises readers to proceed with caution and mindfulness. By choosing to use this book, you accept full responsibility for your actions and any outcomes that may result. The author and publisher disclaim all liability for any harm, loss, or adverse effects that may arise from the use or misuse of this material.

Spiritual and Cultural Respect

This book does not claim to provide historical accuracy or a comprehensive account of the White Witch of Rose Hall's practices or beliefs. Instead, it is a fictional and artistic interpretation inspired by her legendary reputation. The author acknowledges the cultural and historical significance of Rose Hall and the Caribbean's rich heritage and does not intend to exploit or misrepresent these traditions. Readers are encouraged to approach this material with an open mind and a respectful heart, recognizing the complex interplay of history, myth, and modern reinterpretation.

Ethical Use of Spells

The spells and rituals within this book are intended for positive and constructive purposes. They are not designed for harm, manipulation, or coercion. Readers are reminded of the ethical principle that energy sent out into the world often returns to the sender. Misuse of the practices described herein can have serious spiritual, emotional, and even physical consequences. Practitioners are urged to adhere to ethical guidelines and to act with integrity, compassion, and wisdom.

Acknowledgment of Inspiration

This book is inspired by the White Witch of Rose Hall as a symbol of power, mystery, and resilience. It is not an attempt to definitively portray her life, actions, or beliefs. Rather, it is a creative endeavor to celebrate her enduring presence in folklore and to honor her as a figure of strength and individuality.

By reading and using *The White Witch of Rose Hall's Spellbook*, you acknowledge and accept the terms of this disclaimer. May your journey with this book be one of inspiration, respect, and personal growth. Remember, magic is a profound force—handle it with care and reverence.

Introduction to *The White Witch of Rose Hall's Spellbook*

The allure of witchcraft has long captivated the imagination, weaving stories of power, mystery, and the untamed forces of nature. This spellbook serves as both a tribute to one of the most enigmatic figures in the history of witchcraft, Annie Palmer—known as the White Witch of Rose Hall—and a guide for those seeking to understand and practice the craft responsibly and effectively. Within these pages, you will find spells inspired by various traditions, ethical guidance for their use, and a roadmap to harnessing your inner magic.

The Legend of the White Witch

Annie Palmer, famously known as the White Witch of Rose Hall, remains a figure shrouded in myth and intrigue. Born in Haiti and raised amid the mystical practices of Voodoo, Annie later moved to Jamaica, where she became the mistress of the infamous Rose Hall plantation. Her mastery of magical arts, combined with her rumored ruthlessness, earned her the moniker "The White Witch." Tales of her life tell of her beauty, power, and the chilling demise of those who crossed her.

Though historical records paint her in shades of mystery, the legend of the White Witch endures as a testament to her connection to the unseen realms. This spellbook is not an attempt to recount her exact practices but rather a creative homage to her enduring legend. It celebrates her as a symbol of strength, independence, and mystical mastery.

Magic Across Traditions

Magic, in its essence, transcends cultural and geographical boundaries, taking on various forms and interpretations across the world. To understand the spells in this book, it is helpful to recognize the different traditions from which they draw inspiration:

- **Voodoo Magic**: Rooted in African spiritual practices, Voodoo incorporates rituals to connect with spirits, ancestors, and the natural world. It emphasizes balance, community, and respect for the unseen forces that shape our lives.
- **White Magic**: Often associated with healing, protection, and positive energy, white magic focuses on aligning with nature and bringing about harmony. It seeks to uplift and empower without causing harm.
- **Red Magic**: A lesser-known tradition, red magic is tied to passion, desire, and matters of the heart. It harnesses the energy of love and attraction while emphasizing the ethical responsibility of free will.
- **Black Magic**: Considered controversial, black magic deals with the shadow aspects of energy, such as banishing, binding, and defensive spells. While often misunderstood, it has its place in protecting oneself from harm when used with caution and integrity.

This spellbook integrates elements from these traditions, offering a diverse range of practices that honor their origins and unique contributions to the craft.

Ethical Considerations

Magic is a powerful tool, but with power comes responsibility. As you explore the spells in this book, it is crucial to consider the following:

- **Intent Matters**: The energy you channel into a spell is guided by your intent. Approach every spell with clarity, mindfulness, and a sense of purpose. Avoid using magic for manipulation, harm, or revenge.
- **Consequences Are Real**: Magic often works in ways that are unexpected or indirect. Be prepared to accept the outcomes of your actions and understand that what you send out into the world may return to you.
- **Respect the Balance of Nature**: Magic is not about forcing your will upon the universe but working in harmony with natural forces. Respect the cycles of the moon, the seasons, and the energies of the earth as you practice.

By adhering to these principles, you honor the craft, yourself, and the legacy of witches who came before you, including the White Witch of Rose Hall.

How to Use This Spellbook

This spellbook is designed as a practical and spiritual guide for beginners and seasoned practitioners alike. It includes a wide array of spells, rituals, and insights to help you unlock your potential and connect with the energies around you.

- **Choosing a Spell**: Each spell is categorized by purpose, such as protection, love, prosperity, or cleansing. Read through the descriptions carefully to select the one that aligns with your needs and intentions.
- **Preparatory Rituals**: Successful spellcasting begins with preparation. Before performing any spell, take the time to cleanse your space, ground your energy, and focus your mind. This may involve meditation, lighting candles, burning incense, or using sacred tools.
- **Gathering Materials**: Many spells require specific ingredients or tools, such as herbs, crystals, or symbols. Ensure you have everything you need before you begin and handle each item with respect.
- **Performing the Spell**: Follow the instructions provided, but remember that your personal touch is vital. Magic is not about rigid adherence to rules but about channeling your unique energy and intuition.
- **Reflection and Gratitude**: After completing a spell, take time to reflect on the experience. Offer gratitude to the forces you have worked with, whether they are spirits, deities, or natural energies.

This spellbook is more than a collection of spells—it is an invitation to step into your power, honor your spiritual heritage, and connect with the unseen forces that shape our reality. May it guide you on your magical journey and inspire you to approach the craft with the same confidence and mastery that defined the legendary White Witch of Rose Hall.

Welcome to the spellbook. May you tread lightly, act wisely, and cast boldly.

Chapter 1: The Fundamentals of Spellcraft

The practice of spellcraft is as old as humanity itself. Across cultures and centuries, people have sought to connect with the unseen forces of the universe to bring about change, manifest desires, and protect themselves and their loved ones. At its core, spellcraft is about channeling your intention and energy to work in harmony with natural and spiritual forces. Before diving into advanced spells and rituals, it's essential to understand the fundamentals of magical theory, the tools you'll use, and the importance of intention.

Basic Magical Theory

At its heart, magic is the art of transformation. It is the ability to align your personal energy with the greater forces of nature and the universe to influence outcomes. Here are some key concepts:

- **Energy and Vibration**: Everything in the universe carries an energetic signature and vibrates at a particular frequency. Magic works by raising, directing, and transforming energy to align with your desired outcome.
- **The Law of Correspondence**: In magical practice, "as above, so below; as within, so without" is a guiding principle. This means that the energies within you reflect and influence the external world, and vice versa.
- **Intent is Key**: The driving force behind any spell is your intention. A clear, focused intention is more powerful than elaborate rituals or expensive tools. The stronger your belief in your work, the more effective your magic will be.
- **Balance and Respect**: Magic is not about control or dominance. It's about working with, not against, the natural flow of energy. Respect for the forces you work with is paramount to successful spellcraft.

Ingredients and Tools

While your energy and intention are the most important elements in spellcraft, tools and ingredients serve to amplify and focus your power. Each tool and ingredient carries its own energy and symbolism, which can enhance your magic.

Candles

Candles are a staple in spellcraft, representing the element of fire and the power of transformation. Each color carries specific correspondences:

- **White**: Purity, protection, healing.
- **Black**: Banishing, protection, grounding.
- **Green**: Prosperity, growth, abundance.
- **Red**: Passion, courage, vitality.
- **Blue**: Peace, communication, intuition.
- **Yellow**: Joy, creativity, mental clarity. When using candles, anoint them with oil and focus your intention as you light them. The flame symbolizes the spark of your desire and its journey into the universe.

Herbs

Herbs are powerful allies in spellcraft, each carrying unique properties:

- **Lavender**: Peace, relaxation, cleansing.
- **Rosemary**: Protection, memory, purification.
- **Sage**: Cleansing, banishing negativity.
- **Cinnamon**: Prosperity, love, warmth.
- **Basil**: Luck, protection, love. Incorporate herbs into your spells by burning them as incense, brewing them into teas, or using them in sachets and charms.

Crystals

Crystals amplify and focus energy, each with its own vibrational properties:

- **Clear Quartz**: Amplification, clarity, versatility.
- **Amethyst**: Intuition, protection, spiritual growth.
- **Rose Quartz**: Love, healing, emotional balance.
- **Black Tourmaline**: Grounding, protection from negativity.
- **Citrine**: Abundance, confidence, manifesting. Crystals can be held during meditation, placed on altars, or carried as talismans.

Other Tools

- **Athame or Wand**: Used for directing energy during rituals.
- **Chalice**: Represents the element of water and is often used in offerings.
- **Pentacle**: A symbol of protection and the balance of the elements.
- **Incense**: Represents the element of air and is used to purify and raise energy.

Simple Charms for Beginners

To begin your magical journey, it's best to start with simple charms that focus on intention-setting and protection. These are foundational practices that build your confidence and understanding of energy work.

Charm for Intention-Setting

This charm helps you focus your energy and align your thoughts with your goals.

Ingredients:

- A white candle
- A piece of paper and a pen
- A small pouch or jar

Steps:

1. Write your intention clearly on the piece of paper. Be specific and positive. For example, "I attract financial abundance" or "I find inner peace."
2. Light the white candle and hold the paper in your hands, focusing on your intention. Visualize it as though it has already happened.
3. Fold the paper and place it in the pouch or jar. Carry this charm with you as a reminder of your goal.

Protection Charm

This charm creates a protective shield around you or your home.

Ingredients:

- A black candle
- A pinch of salt
- A piece of obsidian or black tourmaline

Steps:

1. Light the black candle and sit quietly, grounding your energy.
2. Sprinkle the salt in a circle around the area you want to protect or hold it in your hands as you visualize a protective barrier forming around you.
3. Hold the obsidian or black tourmaline in your dominant hand and say, "With this charm, I am shielded. Harm cannot enter; peace remains."
4. Place the crystal in your pocket or near your front door to maintain the protective energy.

Conclusion

The fundamentals of spellcraft lie in your ability to connect with your tools, your intention, and the energies around you. By mastering the basics of magical theory, ingredients, and tools, you are laying a solid foundation for more complex rituals and spells. The simple charms provided here are an excellent starting point, allowing you to explore the art of magic with confidence and respect. As you progress through this spellbook, remember that your journey is uniquely yours, and the magic you create is a reflection of your own power and potential.

Chapter 2: Voodoo Spells of Power

Voodoo, often misunderstood and misrepresented, is a spiritual tradition deeply rooted in African heritage, Haitian culture, and the blending of indigenous and European influences. It is a system that honors spirits (known as *loa*), ancestors, and the natural forces that govern our world. Voodoo spells are powerful tools that connect practitioners to these energies, allowing them to influence their lives and circumstances with reverence and purpose. This chapter explores spells derived from Voodoo traditions, including rituals for summoning spirits, ancestor communication, protection, and the creation of poppets, or "voodoo dolls," for specific intentions.

The Essence of Voodoo Magic

Voodoo is not merely a system of spells and rituals but a spiritual framework that emphasizes the interconnectedness of all beings. Practicing Voodoo spells requires understanding and respect for its principles:

- **Connection to the Loa**: The loa are spiritual intermediaries between humans and the divine, each with unique attributes and purposes. Building a relationship with the loa through offerings, rituals, and respect is essential for successful spellwork.
- **The Role of Ancestors**: Ancestral spirits play a central role in Voodoo, guiding and protecting their descendants. Honoring them with altars, offerings, and communication rituals strengthens this bond.
- **Balance and Harmony**: Voodoo teaches the importance of living in harmony with nature and the spirit world. Misusing its practices for harm or selfish gain disrupts this balance and invites negative consequences.

Spells and Rituals from Voodoo Traditions

The following spells and rituals are drawn from Voodoo practices, adapted for those seeking to work with its energies respectfully. Always approach these spells with sincerity, preparation, and a clear intention.

1. Ritual for Summoning Spirits

This ritual calls upon a loa or ancestral spirit to guide and assist you. Before performing this ritual, research the loa you wish to summon and their preferences for offerings.

Ingredients:

- A white candle
- A small offering (such as rum, coins, or food)
- Incense (frankincense or sandalwood works well)
- A personal token (an object meaningful to you)

Steps:

1. Create a sacred space where you will not be disturbed. Place the candle and offering in the center.
2. Light the candle and incense, focusing your energy on the spirit you wish to summon.
3. Recite the following invocation (modify for the specific spirit or ancestor): *"Great [name of spirit], I call upon you with respect and gratitude.*
   Hear my plea and come forth,
   Guide me with your wisdom and protect me with your strength.
   I offer this token of my sincerity and devotion.
   Accept it and bless me with your presence."
4. Place your personal token near the offering as a sign of your dedication.

5. Sit quietly and observe any sensations, thoughts, or signs that indicate the spirit's presence. If you feel a connection, express your gratitude and state your request.

6. Thank the spirit and extinguish the candle when you feel the ritual is complete.

2. Ancestor Communication Spell

This spell helps you connect with your ancestors to seek their guidance or blessings.

Ingredients:

- A photo or personal item of the ancestor
- A bowl of water
- A small piece of bread or fruit
- A white cloth or altar cloth

Steps:

1. Set up an altar or sacred space using the white cloth. Place the photo or item of the ancestor at the center.

2. Fill the bowl with water and place it on the altar as a medium for communication.

3. Light a candle (optional) and say: *"Beloved ancestor(s), I call upon you.*
   Through this water, may our connection be clear.
   Hear my words, guide my path, and bless me with your wisdom."

4. Place the bread or fruit as an offering, asking for their assistance or simply expressing gratitude.

5. Meditate or sit quietly, focusing on the ancestor's image. Pay attention to any impressions or thoughts that come to you.

6. When you're done, thank your ancestors and either consume or bury the offering as a sign of respect.

3. Protection Spell Using a Voodoo Doll

A voodoo doll, or poppet, can be used to create a strong protective energy around yourself or someone you care about.

Ingredients:

- A small piece of cloth (preferably white or blue)
- Cotton or herbs for stuffing (such as lavender or rosemary)
- A strand of your hair or personal item
- A needle and thread
- A small piece of paper and pen

Steps:

1. Cut the cloth into the shape of a small human figure and sew the edges together, leaving a small opening for stuffing.
2. Stuff the doll with cotton or herbs, adding your hair or personal item inside to link it to you. Close the opening with stitches.
3. Write your name or the name of the person the doll is protecting on the paper and tuck it inside the doll.
4. Hold the doll and say: *"Guardian spirits, infuse this figure with your strength.*
   Shield me (or name) from harm, negativity, and danger.
   May this doll be a vessel of safety and peace."
5. Keep the doll in a safe place, such as near your bed or on an altar.

4. Voodoo Doll for Love

This spell helps attract positive love energy into your life. Remember to always respect the free will of others when performing love magic.

Ingredients:

- A piece of pink or red cloth
- Cotton or herbs (rose petals or cinnamon)
- A small heart-shaped charm
- A needle and thread
- Personal items (optional: a hair strand or photo)

Steps:

1. Create a poppet as described in the previous spell, but use pink or red cloth.
2. Stuff the doll with the herbs and place the heart-shaped charm inside as a symbol of love.
3. If you have a specific person in mind (who consents), add their item; otherwise, leave the doll neutral to attract the right energy.
4. Hold the doll and visualize the kind of love you want—whether it's self-love, a partner, or improving an existing relationship.
5. Say: *"Spirits of love and harmony,*
   Fill this figure with warmth and passion.
   May love find its way to me,
   Pure and joyful as it's meant to be."
6. Keep the doll near your heart or place it on your altar as a reminder of your intention.

The Ethics of Voodoo Magic

As powerful as Voodoo spells are, it is crucial to use them with care, respect, and ethical consideration. Misusing these practices can lead to unintended consequences. Always act with integrity and remember that the loa and spirits demand respect. Offer gratitude for their assistance and remain mindful of the energies you invoke.

By following these practices, you will build a strong foundation in Voodoo magic, allowing you to connect with its powerful energies while honoring the traditions from which they come.

Chapter 3: White Magic for Healing and Harmony

White magic is a practice deeply rooted in positive intention and the desire to create balance, heal wounds, and foster peace. It seeks to align with the forces of light and nature, focusing on physical and emotional well-being, protecting loved ones, and cultivating harmony in all aspects of life. This chapter explores the use of white magic for healing and harmony, offering spells, blessings, and charms designed to uplift, restore, and balance energy.

The Principles of White Magic

White magic is often referred to as the magic of light, emphasizing its connection to healing, purity, and positive transformation. Practitioners of white magic recognize that:

1. **Healing is Holistic**: True healing addresses the mind, body, and spirit. White magic supports this by channeling energy that restores balance on all levels.
2. **Intent is Everything**: The success of any spell depends on the clarity and purity of the caster's intent. Healing and harmony can only flourish when the practitioner acts with compassion and sincerity.
3. **Nature as an Ally**: White magic draws heavily from the natural world, using herbs, crystals, and elemental forces to amplify its effects.
4. **Respect the Flow of Energy**: White magic does not force outcomes but gently aligns energies to create positive change. It respects free will and the natural rhythms of the universe.

Spells for Physical and Emotional Healing

Healing spells in white magic are designed to soothe pain, boost recovery, and restore emotional well-being. Below are a few spells to begin your healing practice.

1. Healing Light Ritual

This ritual uses the visualization of light to promote physical or emotional healing.

Ingredients:

- A white candle
- Lavender essential oil
- A piece of clear quartz or amethyst

Steps:

1. Find a quiet space where you can relax. Anoint the white candle with lavender oil to infuse it with calming energy.
2. Light the candle and hold the quartz or amethyst in your hands. Close your eyes and take a few deep breaths.
3. Visualize a soft, golden light surrounding you (or the person you wish to heal). Imagine the light entering the body, dissolving pain, and filling every cell with warmth and vitality.
4. Say aloud or silently: *"By the light of healing, may all pain fade. Strength return, and balance be made.*
   With gratitude, I welcome this glow.
   Health and harmony, may they grow."
5. Meditate on this visualization for 10–15 minutes, then extinguish the candle.

2. Emotional Wound Soothing Spell

This spell helps release emotional pain and promotes inner peace.

Ingredients:

- A pink candle (for emotional healing)
- Rose petals or rose quartz
- A small bowl of water

Steps:

1. Place the pink candle in front of you and scatter the rose petals or place the rose quartz around it.
2. Light the candle and hold your hands over the bowl of water, imagining it being filled with soothing energy.
3. Focus on the pain or emotion you wish to release. Speak your intention: *"Waters pure, cleanse my heart.*
   From sorrow and pain, let me depart.
   Fill this space with love and peace.
   From this moment, let all anguish cease."
4. Dip your fingers into the water and gently touch your forehead, heart, and wrists as a symbolic cleansing.
5. Allow the candle to burn out safely or extinguish it when you feel ready.

Blessings for Home and Family

The home is a sacred space, and family is a source of strength and love. These blessings ensure protection, warmth, and harmony within your living space and among loved ones.

1. Home Blessing Ritual

This ritual purifies your home and fills it with positive energy.

Ingredients:

- Sage or palo santo for smudging
- A white candle
- A bowl of salt water
- Fresh flowers or herbs (e.g., rosemary, basil)

Steps:

1. Begin by smudging your home with sage or palo santo, moving clockwise from the front door through each room. As you smudge, say: *"I cleanse this space of all that's old.*
   Only light and love may hold."
2. Place the white candle in a central location and light it. Sprinkle salt water around the home, focusing on doorways and windows.
3. Arrange the fresh flowers or herbs in a vase to symbolize growth and positivity.
4. Conclude with: *"Bless this home, let joy reside.*
   Within these walls, let love abide."
5. Allow the candle to burn as long as is safe.

2. Family Harmony Blessing

This spell strengthens bonds and resolves tension within the family.

Ingredients:

- A green or blue candle
- A family photo or symbolic item
- Chamomile tea (optional)

Steps:

1. Gather the candle, photo, and any family members willing to participate. If they cannot, visualize them clearly in your mind.
2. Light the candle and place the photo in front of it. Say: *"Together we stand, as one we grow.*
   Peace and love, let them flow.
   Harmony reign in this family of mine,
   With every breath, let our hearts align."
3. Share chamomile tea or spend a moment reflecting on positive memories as a family.

Charms for Harmony, Peace, and Tranquility

Charms are simple yet powerful tools to attract and maintain a sense of balance and calm.

1. Peaceful Sleep Charm

This charm helps ensure restful sleep and relieves nighttime anxiety.

Ingredients:

- A small sachet or pouch
- Lavender and chamomile (dried)
- A small piece of moonstone

Steps:

1. Fill the sachet with lavender, chamomile, and the moonstone.
2. Hold the sachet in your hands and say: *"By the moon's soft light, I call for peace.*
   Let my worries and fears release.
   As I lay down, let my mind rest.
   Peaceful sleep, I am blessed."
3. Place the sachet under your pillow or beside your bed.

2. Harmony Charm for Relationships

This charm promotes understanding and balance in personal relationships.

Ingredients:

- A piece of blue ribbon
- Two small rose quartz stones
- A sprig of rosemary

Steps:

1. Tie the two rose quartz stones together with the blue ribbon, adding the rosemary to the knot.
2. Hold the charm and focus on the relationship you wish to improve, saying: *"By stone and herb, let hearts align.*
   Harmony flow, pure and divine.
   May love and peace replace despair,
   This bond is strong; this bond is fair."
3. Keep the charm in a safe place where it won't be disturbed.

Conclusion

White magic is a gentle yet profound practice that seeks to heal, protect, and harmonize. Whether you are working on physical recovery, emotional well-being, or creating a sanctuary for your loved ones, the spells, blessings, and charms in this chapter provide a foundation for bringing light and balance into your life. Approach these practices with sincerity, and remember that the true essence of white magic lies in your positive intentions and the love you infuse into your work.

Chapter 4: Red Magic: Spells of Passion and Desire

Red magic, often referred to as the magic of passion, focuses on matters of the heart, desire, and emotional intensity. Rooted in the fiery energy of love and attraction, it can be a powerful force for creating deep connections, reigniting romance, and strengthening emotional bonds. Red magic celebrates the raw power of emotions and the beauty of intimacy, but it must be approached with care, respect, and ethical intent to honor the free will of all involved.

The Essence of Red Magic

Red magic draws upon the energy of the heart and the primal forces of love and attraction. It is associated with the element of fire and the planet Venus, both symbolic of vitality, desire, and beauty. Key principles to keep in mind when practicing red magic include:

- **Respect for Free Will**: Love magic must never force someone's feelings or manipulate their will. Instead, it should enhance mutual feelings, attract like-minded individuals, or deepen existing bonds.
- **The Power of Self-Love**: Red magic is most effective when the practitioner is grounded in self-love and confidence. Before casting spells for others, ensure your own emotional foundation is strong.
- **Passion as Energy**: Passion is the driving force of red magic. Channeling this energy requires focus and a clear understanding of your desires.

Love Potions and Attraction Spells

Love potions and attraction spells are some of the oldest and most popular forms of red magic. They are used to enhance your natural charm, draw love into your life, or deepen a romantic connection.

1. Attraction Oil

This oil can be used to anoint candles, objects, or even yourself to enhance your natural allure and draw love or admiration.

Ingredients:

- A small glass vial or bottle
- Carrier oil (such as almond or jojoba oil)
- Essential oils: rose, jasmine, and cinnamon
- Dried rose petals
- A small garnet or rose quartz crystal

Steps:

1. Fill the glass vial with the carrier oil, leaving some space at the top.
2. Add a few drops each of rose, jasmine, and cinnamon essential oils.
3. Place the dried rose petals and the crystal inside the vial.
4. Seal the vial and hold it in your hands, focusing on your intention. Say: *"By rose and flame, my charm does rise.*
   Love and passion drawn to my eyes.
   With this oil, I call to me,
   The energy of love, pure and free."
5. Use this oil to anoint candles during love spells, wear a small amount on your pulse points, or add a drop to a bath.

2. Simple Love Attraction Spell

This spell attracts love into your life by amplifying your natural energy and radiance.

Ingredients:

- A pink or red candle
- A small mirror
- A piece of rose quartz

Steps:

1. Light the pink or red candle and place the mirror in front of it so the flame is reflected.
2. Hold the rose quartz in your hands and gaze into the mirror. Visualize yourself surrounded by a warm, loving light, radiating confidence and charm.
3. Say: *"Flame of passion, light of love,*
   Draw to me what I dream of.
   A heart that's true, a soul that's kind,
   A love that's pure, and perfectly aligned."
4. Carry the rose quartz with you as a talisman to attract love.

Charms for Enhancing Romance and Passion

Red magic charms are designed to reignite the spark in a relationship or create an atmosphere of romance and sensuality.

1. Passion Charm Sachet

This charm enhances romance and intimacy between partners.

Ingredients:

- A small red or pink sachet or pouch
- Dried rose petals
- Cinnamon sticks
- A few drops of patchouli or ylang-ylang essential oil
- A strand of hair or personal item from each partner (optional)

Steps:

1. Fill the sachet with rose petals, cinnamon sticks, and the optional personal items.
2. Add a few drops of the essential oil to the sachet and tie it closed.
3. Hold the sachet in your hands with your partner (if possible) and say: *"By fire's warmth and passion's glow,*
   Let our love continue to grow.
   With this charm, our bond is sealed,
   A love so deep, it is revealed."
4. Keep the sachet in your bedroom to maintain the romantic energy.

2. Candle Ritual for Rekindling Passion

This ritual is perfect for couples who want to reignite the flame of romance.

Ingredients:

- Two red candles
- A piece of red string
- A small dish of honey

Steps:

1. Place the two red candles close together and tie them loosely with the red string.
2. Light the candles and dip your fingers into the honey. Taste the honey and offer some to your partner, symbolizing the sweetness of your connection.
3. Say together: *"Flames of passion, burn so bright,*
   Rekindle love in the softest light.
   Sweet as honey, our bond shall be,
   Strong and lasting, eternally."
4. Let the candles burn safely for a while before extinguishing them.

Spells for Strengthening Emotional Bonds

These spells are designed to deepen trust, communication, and emotional intimacy in relationships.

1. Bonding Spell

This spell strengthens the emotional connection between two people.

Ingredients:

- A white candle
- A red ribbon
- A small piece of paper
- A pen

Steps:

1. Write your name and the name of the other person on the piece of paper. Draw a heart around the names.
2. Tie the red ribbon around the paper while focusing on your intention to strengthen your bond.
3. Light the white candle and say: *"By this flame, our hearts entwine, A bond of trust, forever divine. Stronger with each passing day, Love and care shall guide our way."*
4. Keep the ribbon-wrapped paper in a safe place as a reminder of your commitment.

2. Heart-to-Heart Communication Spell

This spell fosters open communication and understanding between partners.

Ingredients:

- Two blue candles
- A piece of paper
- A pen
- A small bowl of water

Steps:

1. Light the two blue candles and place them on either side of the bowl of water.
2. Write your feelings or concerns on the piece of paper, being honest and clear.
3. Hold the paper over the water and say: *"Water clear, let truth flow.*
   Let understanding and kindness grow.
   With open hearts, we shall speak,
   Building bonds strong, not weak."
4. Submerge the paper in the water, symbolizing the cleansing of miscommunication. Dispose of the paper and water respectfully.

Conclusion

Red magic celebrates the beauty of love, passion, and emotional connection. Whether you are seeking new love, deepening an existing bond, or igniting romance, the spells and charms in this chapter provide practical and heartfelt ways to channel your desires. Remember that love begins with self-respect and sincerity, and the energy you put into your magic will ripple back to you. Use red magic wisely and with an open heart, and it will guide you to fulfilling and meaningful connections.

Chapter 5: Black Magic for Defense and Retribution

Black magic, often misunderstood and feared, is a potent form of energy work that focuses on shadow aspects of the self and the environment. It is not inherently evil but must be approached with care, respect, and ethical consideration. In this chapter, we explore the practical applications of black magic for defense, retribution, and banishment. These spells are powerful tools to protect against harm, remove toxic influences, and, when absolutely necessary, seek justice through retributive magic.

Understanding Black Magic

Black magic operates in the darker realms of energy, addressing threats, harm, and negativity. While its power can be immense, it carries a heavy responsibility. Before engaging in black magic, keep the following in mind:

1. **Intent is Crucial**: Your motivation should always be clear and justified. Black magic is not for petty revenge or manipulation—it is for defense, protection, and setting strong boundaries.
2. **The Rule of Return**: Energies you send out may return to you, sometimes magnified. This principle is why practitioners are advised to act with fairness and integrity.
3. **Consent of the Spirit World**: Black magic often involves working with spirits or forces that must be approached with respect. Neglecting this can lead to unintended consequences.

Protection Spells Using Darker Energies

Black magic excels in creating barriers against harm and shielding the practitioner from malicious forces.

1. Shadow Shield Spell

This spell creates a protective barrier of shadow energy around you, deflecting harm and negativity.

Ingredients:

- A black candle
- A piece of obsidian or onyx
- A pinch of salt
- A small mirror

Steps:

1. Sit in a quiet, dimly lit space. Place the black candle, mirror, and obsidian before you in a triangle formation, with the candle at the apex.
2. Light the candle and sprinkle the salt in a circle around your space for protection.
3. Hold the obsidian in your hand and gaze into the mirror. Visualize a swirling vortex of shadows enveloping you, forming a shield.
4. Chant: *"Shadows rise, and shadows fall.*
   Protect me now; deflect it all.
   No harm shall pass, no ill shall stay.
   By this shield, I keep harm away."
5. Meditate on this protective energy for a few moments, then extinguish the candle.

2. Binding Spell for Protection

This spell prevents a specific person from causing harm without inflicting unnecessary suffering.

Ingredients:

- A black ribbon or cord
- A small piece of paper and a pen
- A black candle

Steps:

1. Write the name of the person you wish to bind on the paper. Fold it three times.
2. Wrap the paper tightly with the black ribbon, focusing on your intent to stop their harmful actions.
3. Light the black candle and say: *"Bound by ribbon, bound by will, Your harm ends now; your hand is still. No more shall you inflict despair. My will is strong, this bond is fair."*
4. Store the bound paper in a safe place, such as a box or jar, until you feel the binding is no longer necessary. Dispose of it respectfully when the bond is released.

Curses and Hexes for Retribution

Curses and hexes are serious magical actions that should be undertaken only when justice is necessary and all other avenues have been exhausted. Always weigh the potential consequences and ensure your intent is justifiable.

1. The Mirror Curse

This curse reflects harm or negativity back to its source.

Ingredients:

- A small mirror
- A black cloth
- A piece of black string

Steps:

1. Write the name of the person causing harm on the back of the mirror.
2. Wrap the mirror in the black cloth, symbolizing their harm being returned to them.
3. Tie the black string around the cloth and say: *"What you send shall now reflect.*
   Harm returns; your deeds collect.
   By this curse, your actions cease.
   I call for justice, balance, and peace."
4. Store the mirror in a hidden place or bury it away from your home. This ensures the curse takes effect while keeping your energy clear.

2. The Thorn Hex

This hex creates a barrier of discomfort for someone who has caused harm, deterring further actions.

Ingredients:

- A thorny branch or dried thorns
- A black candle
- A piece of paper and pen

Steps:

1. Write the person's name on the paper along with their harmful actions. Roll the paper tightly and wrap it in the thorny branch.
2. Light the black candle and hold the thorn bundle over it (safely, without burning it). Say: *"Thorns of justice, sharp and keen,*
   Protect the innocent, remain unseen.
   Your harm is ended, your deeds returned.
   Let this lesson now be learned."
3. Bury the bundle far from your home to complete the hex.

Spells for Banishing Negative Entities or Toxic Influences

Banishing spells are among the most important applications of black magic. They remove harmful energies, entities, or individuals from your life.

1. Banishing Ritual for Negative Entities

This ritual expels malevolent spirits or energies from your space.

Ingredients:

- A black candle
- Sage or palo santo for smudging
- A bowl of salt water
- A piece of onyx or hematite

Steps:

1. Light the black candle and smudge your space with sage or palo santo to cleanse it.
2. Sprinkle salt water around your home, focusing on areas where negativity is strongest.
3. Hold the onyx or hematite and say: *"Spirit of shadow, spirit of light,*
   I cast you out, away from my sight.
   This space is sacred; it is mine.
   Leave now, and cross no line."
4. Place the stone near an entry point (such as a door or window) to maintain the protective barrier.

2. Toxic Influence Banishing Spell

This spell removes a toxic person or influence from your life.

Ingredients:

- A black candle
- A piece of paper and pen
- A fireproof bowl or cauldron

Steps:

1. Write the name of the person or influence on the paper. Focus on your desire to remove them from your life.
2. Light the black candle and hold the paper over the flame, allowing it to catch fire safely. Drop it into the fireproof bowl.
3. As the paper burns, say: *"By fire's might, I cast you away.*
   Your power fades with each passing day.
   No longer shall your shadow fall;
   You are banished—gone from it all."
4. Dispose of the ashes outside, far from your home, to finalize the spell.

Ethical Considerations for Black Magic

Black magic requires maturity, respect, and a deep understanding of its consequences. Keep these guidelines in mind:

- **Self-Reflection**: Before casting, ask yourself if the spell is truly necessary and justified.
- **Protection**: Always shield yourself before and after performing black magic to avoid unintended consequences.
- **Closure**: Once a spell is complete, release the energy and move forward without dwelling on the situation.

Conclusion

Black magic, when used responsibly, is a powerful tool for defense, retribution, and banishment. It allows practitioners to reclaim their power and protect themselves from harm. However, it is not to be wielded lightly. Approach every spell with clarity, caution, and respect for the balance of energy. In doing so, you honor the craft and ensure its power serves justice, protection, and peace.

Chapter 6: The Art of Servitor and Thought-Form Creation

Servitors, also known as thought-forms, are powerful magical constructs created by practitioners to perform specific tasks or fulfill unique purposes. They are a product of focused intention, energy, and visualization, imbued with life-like attributes to serve their creator. Unlike spirits or deities, servitors are entirely artificial entities designed to operate within the boundaries set by their creator. This chapter provides a detailed guide on creating, maintaining, and working with servitors, covering their purpose, feeding, housing, appearance, and sigil crafting.

What Are Servitors?

A servitor is an energetic construct created to carry out a task or embody a specific quality. Unlike autonomous spirits, servitors are bound to their creator's will and purpose. They can be programmed for a variety of roles, such as protection, healing, guidance, or attracting opportunities.

- **Purpose**: Servitors are created with a single or narrow range of purposes, defined clearly during their creation.
- **Temporary or Permanent**: Some servitors are designed for short-term tasks and dissolve afterward, while others are long-term and require regular upkeep.

Steps to Create a Servitor

Creating a servitor involves several deliberate steps. Each phase of creation requires focus, intention, and clarity to ensure the servitor functions as intended.

Step 1: Define the Purpose

The first step in creating a servitor is deciding its purpose. Be as specific as possible. A well-defined purpose ensures the servitor operates effectively without confusion.

Examples of purposes:

- Protection: Guard your home or energy field from harm.
- Healing: Assist in physical or emotional recovery.
- Motivation: Inspire focus and productivity for creative projects.
- Wealth: Attract opportunities for financial growth.

Write the purpose in a clear, concise statement. For example:
"This servitor's purpose is to protect me from negative energy and psychic attacks."

Step 2: Design the Appearance

Visualizing your servitor's form helps solidify its existence in your mind and the astral realm. Its appearance can be symbolic or functional, depending on its purpose.

- **Humanoid**: A warrior for protection, a healer for recovery.
- **Animal-like**: A fox for cunning, a lion for strength.
- **Abstract**: A glowing orb, a shadowy mist, or a crystalline figure.

Sketch or write a detailed description of the servitor's appearance. Include details like color, size, texture, and movement.

Step 3: Create a Sigil

The sigil acts as the servitor's energetic anchor and identifier. It is a symbol that embodies the servitor's purpose and connects it to the physical world.

How to Create the Sigil:

1. Write down the servitor's purpose as a statement. For example: *"Protect my energy field from harm."*
2. Remove repeating letters to create a unique sequence. Example: *Protect my energy field from harm → PRCTMYNGE-FLDH*
3. Rearrange and stylize the remaining letters into a symbol.
4. Refine the design into something visually distinct.

Draw the final sigil on paper, parchment, or a dedicated item (such as a stone or piece of jewelry).

Step 4: Construct the Servitor

Now that you've defined the purpose, appearance, and sigil, it's time to breathe life into your servitor.

Steps:

1. **Set the Stage**: Create a ritual space with candles, incense, and any tools or objects that symbolize the servitor's purpose.
2. **Focus Energy**: Sit quietly and meditate, visualizing a sphere of energy between your hands. Imagine this energy as raw, unshaped potential.
3. **Build the Form**: Begin shaping the energy into the servitor's form as you've envisioned it. Visualize its appearance vividly.
4. **Imbue the Sigil**: Hold the sigil and focus your intention. Say aloud:
   "By my will, I create you. You are [servitor's name], and your purpose is [state purpose]. You are bound to my will and to this sigil. So it is."

5. **Seal the Bond**: Place the sigil where the servitor can "reside" or use it as a focus for activating the servitor.

Feeding and Maintaining a Servitor

Servitors require energy to sustain themselves, especially if they are long-term constructs. Feeding a servitor ensures it remains effective and functional.

- **Energy Sources**: Feed your servitor through visualization, offerings, or specific rituals. For example:
    - Visualize a stream of light transferring energy to the servitor.
    - Light a candle and dedicate its flame to energizing the servitor.
- **Offerings**: For servitors with symbolic associations (e.g., wealth), offer items that align with their purpose, such as coins or crystals.

Regularly check on your servitor during meditation to ensure it is functioning as intended.

Creating a Home for Your Servitor

A servitor's "home" serves as its resting place and energetic anchor. This can be physical or symbolic.

- **Physical Home**: Use a small box, jar, or object (e.g., a statue or gemstone) as the servitor's vessel. Place the sigil inside or attach it to the object.
- **Astral Home**: If you prefer, visualize an astral sanctuary for your servitor—a location where it can retreat when not in use.

Activating and Deploying a Servitor

Once created, your servitor can be activated and deployed for its purpose.

1. **Activation**: Hold the sigil or focus on the servitor's home and say:
   "[Name], awaken and fulfill your purpose. Protect/heal/guide me as I command."
2. **Deployment**: Visualize the servitor moving into action. For example:
   - A protective servitor surrounding you with a shield.
   - A guiding servitor whispering intuitive insights.

Deactivating and Dissolving a Servitor

If a servitor has completed its purpose or is no longer needed, it's essential to deactivate and dissolve it responsibly.

Steps:

1. Call the servitor back to its sigil or home.
2. Thank it for its service and say: *"Your purpose is complete. I release you from my service. Return to the energy from which you were formed."*
3. Visualize the servitor dissolving into light or dissipating into the universe.
4. Destroy or cleanse the sigil or object, ensuring no lingering energy remains.

Ethical Considerations

While servitors are bound to your will, they are energetic constructs deserving of respect. Follow these ethical guidelines:

- **Do No Harm**: Avoid creating servitors for malicious or harmful purposes, as the energy may rebound on you.
- **Purposeful Creation**: Do not create servitors frivolously or without a clear need.
- **Maintain Boundaries**: Always set limits on your servitor's autonomy to prevent unintended consequences.

Conclusion

The creation of servitors and thought-forms is a profound act of magical artistry and responsibility. By following the steps outlined in this chapter, you can design powerful, focused entities to assist you in your magical practice and daily life. Whether for protection, guidance, or manifestation, servitors are invaluable allies—if treated with respect and maintained with care. As you hone your skills, the possibilities for servitor creation are limited only by your imagination and intent.

Chapter 7: Nature's Secrets: Herbal and Plant Magic

Nature has always been a profound source of magical power. Herbs, flowers, and plants carry unique energies and properties, making them indispensable tools for spellcraft. In this chapter, we delve into the secrets of herbal and plant magic, focusing on the flora that might have thrived around Rose Hall and its mystical surroundings. You will learn to create potions, tinctures, and elixirs for healing, protection, attraction, and more.

The Power of Nature in Magic

Herbs and plants have been used in magical practices for centuries, valued for their symbolic and energetic properties. Their essence can be harnessed in spells, rituals, and remedies to align with natural forces and manifest intentions.

- **Energetic Correspondences**: Each herb or plant carries a unique vibrational frequency that resonates with specific magical purposes.
- **Symbiotic Relationship**: Working with herbs creates a deeper connection with nature and its cycles, grounding your magic in the natural world.
- **Simplicity and Accessibility**: Many powerful herbs and plants can be found in your surroundings, making herbal magic both practical and effective.

The Plants of Rose Hall

The lush tropical surroundings of Rose Hall provide an abundant source of plants traditionally associated with Caribbean magic and folklore. Some of these may include:

- **Rosemary**: Found near gardens, this herb is associated with memory, protection, and purification.
- **Basil**: A staple in the Caribbean, basil is linked to love, prosperity, and protection.
- **Hibiscus**: These vibrant flowers are used for love, passion, and divination.
- **Coconut Palm**: The coconut and its oil are symbols of purification and spiritual cleansing.
- **Allspice**: Native to the region, this spice is associated with abundance, healing, and vitality.
- **Aloe Vera**: A common plant with powerful healing and protective qualities.

Spells Using Herbs, Flowers, and Plants

Herbs and plants can be used in their raw form or transformed into magical preparations such as potions, tinctures, and elixirs. Below are some spells that utilize their power.

1. Healing Balm with Aloe Vera

Aloe vera is renowned for its soothing and healing properties, making it ideal for creating a magical balm.

Ingredients:

- A fresh aloe vera leaf
- Coconut oil
- A pinch of dried lavender (optional)
- A small jar

Steps:

1. Slice the aloe vera leaf and scoop out the gel into a bowl.
2. Mix the gel with melted coconut oil and add a pinch of dried lavender for added healing energy.
3. While mixing, say: *"From nature's heart, I draw this balm,*
   To heal and soothe, to bring me calm.
   With love and light, this magic flows,
   Healing power, as nature knows."
4. Store the balm in a jar and use it on minor cuts, burns, or irritated skin.

2. Protective Garden Spell

This spell uses herbs and plants to create a barrier of protection around your home.

Ingredients:

- Rosemary
- Basil
- Lavender
- A small pouch or gardening tools

Steps:

1. Plant rosemary, basil, and lavender around the perimeter of your home or in pots near entryways.
2. As you plant, recite: *"By earth and root, by leaf and bloom,*
   Protect this space, dispel all gloom.
   No harm may enter, no ill may stay,
   Shield this home both night and day."
3. Water the plants regularly, thanking them for their protective energy.

3. Love and Attraction Spell with Hibiscus

Hibiscus flowers, with their vibrant energy, are ideal for enhancing love and passion.

Ingredients:

- A handful of hibiscus petals
- Rose petals
- A pink or red candle
- A small bottle or jar

Steps:

1. Boil the hibiscus and rose petals in water to create a love-infused potion. Let it cool and strain it into a jar.
2. Light the candle and hold the jar, focusing on your intention to attract love or deepen passion.
3. Say: *"Flowers of love, bold and true,*
   Bring passion's fire and connection anew.
   With open heart, I call to thee,
   A love that's pure and meant for me."
4. Use the potion to anoint yourself (on your wrists or heart) or place a few drops in a bath for a love-drawing ritual.

Creating Potions, Tinctures, and Elixirs

Potions, tinctures, and elixirs are powerful ways to harness the magical properties of plants. Each preparation method is suited to specific purposes and uses.

1. Potions

Potions are liquid mixtures charged with magical energy. They can be consumed (if safe) or used externally.

Example: Peaceful Sleep Potion

- Ingredients: Chamomile flowers, lavender, honey.
- Steps: Brew chamomile and lavender in hot water. Add a spoonful of honey and stir clockwise, focusing on calm and restful energy. Drink before bed to encourage peaceful sleep.

2. Tinctures

Tinctures are concentrated herbal extracts made with alcohol or vinegar. They are ideal for long-term storage.

Example: Protection Tincture

- Ingredients: Rosemary, basil, vodka (or apple cider vinegar for non-alcoholic tinctures).
- Steps: Place the herbs in a jar and cover with vodka or vinegar. Seal tightly and let sit for 4–6 weeks, shaking occasionally. Strain and store in a dark bottle. Use a few drops to anoint objects or yourself for protection.

3. Elixirs

Elixirs are potions infused with additional sweeteners or spirits, often used for emotional or spiritual healing.

Example: Heart Healing Elixir

- Ingredients: Rose petals, honey, brandy.
- Steps: Steep rose petals in hot water to create a tea. Mix the tea with honey and a splash of brandy. Use for emotional healing by taking a small sip during meditation or rituals.

Crafting Herbal Amulets and Sachets

In addition to liquid preparations, herbs can be used in solid forms like amulets or sachets.

- **Protection Sachet**: Fill a small pouch with rosemary, basil, and salt. Carry it in your bag or place it near your bed for protection.
- **Love Amulet**: Place rose petals, a piece of cinnamon stick, and a rose quartz in a red cloth. Tie it with a pink ribbon and wear or carry it to attract love.

Ethical Harvesting and Gratitude

When working with plants, it's important to respect the natural world:

- **Sustainable Harvesting**: Take only what you need and ensure the plant's survival.
- **Gratitude Offerings**: Leave an offering (such as a small coin, water, or a whispered thanks) to honor the plant's spirit.
- **Cleansing and Blessing**: Before using herbs, cleanse them by passing them through smoke or sprinkling them with water. Bless them with your intention to amplify their power.

Conclusion

Herbs, flowers, and plants hold the wisdom and energy of nature, offering endless possibilities for magical practice. By incorporating these gifts of the earth into your spells, potions, and rituals, you create a bridge between the mundane and the mystical. Approach their use with respect and gratitude, and they will reward you with their potent and transformative energies. May the secrets of nature guide your path and empower your craft.

Chapter 8: Elemental Magic: Harnessing Earth, Water, Fire, and Air

Elemental magic is one of the oldest and most profound forms of spellcraft, rooted in the belief that the natural elements—Earth, Water, Fire, and Air—are the fundamental forces shaping the universe. By working with these elements, practitioners can harness their unique energies for spells, rituals, and charms to achieve harmony, balance, and transformation. This chapter explores the power of elemental magic, offering detailed spells and rituals for invoking these forces, as well as techniques for weather control, fertility, purification, and connection with nature.

The Elements in Magic

Each element represents a distinct energy and quality, associated with specific magical purposes and correspondences:

1. **Earth**: Stability, fertility, grounding, abundance.
    - Symbol: Soil, stones, plants.
    - Direction: North.
    - Season: Winter.
    - Color: Green or brown.
    - Tools: Salt, crystals, pentacles.
2. **Water**: Emotion, intuition, healing, purification.
    - Symbol: Rivers, seas, cups.
    - Direction: West.
    - Season: Autumn.
    - Color: Blue or silver.
    - Tools: Chalices, bowls, shells.
3. **Fire**: Passion, transformation, energy, destruction.

- Symbol: Flames, candles, lava.
- Direction: South.
- Season: Summer.
- Color: Red, orange, or gold.
- Tools: Candles, wands, athames.

4. **Air**: Thought, communication, intellect, movement.
   - Symbol: Wind, feathers, incense.
   - Direction: East.
   - Season: Spring.
   - Color: Yellow or white.
   - Tools: Incense, bells, fans.

By invoking the elements, practitioners can align themselves with the forces of nature, calling upon these energies to enhance their spellwork.

Spells Invoking the Elements

The following spells are designed to invoke the elements and channel their energies for specific purposes.

1. Earth Invocation Spell for Grounding and Abundance

This spell draws on the stabilizing and nurturing energy of Earth to ground your spirit and attract prosperity.

Ingredients:

- A bowl of soil or sand
- A green or brown candle
- A small stone or crystal (e.g., moss agate or pyrite)

Steps:

1. Place the soil, candle, and crystal in a circle around you.
2. Light the candle and hold the crystal in your hands.
3. Say: *"Spirit of Earth, strong and true,*
   Ground me now, and see me through.

> *Bring stability, abundance, and care,*
> *Your fertile energy, everywhere."*

4. Visualize roots extending from your body into the soil, anchoring you to the Earth's energy.
5. Keep the crystal as a talisman for abundance.

2. Water Invocation Spell for Healing and Emotional Release

This spell uses Water's cleansing and soothing energy to heal emotional wounds.

Ingredients:

- A bowl of water
- A blue candle
- A few drops of lavender oil

Steps:

1. Add the lavender oil to the water and place it in front of you alongside the blue candle.
2. Light the candle and dip your fingers into the water, feeling its cool energy.
3. Say: *"Spirit of Water, calm and deep,*
   Heal my heart, where sorrows seep.
   Wash away the pain I bear,
   Bring me peace, beyond compare."
4. Gently anoint your forehead, heart, and wrists with the water.
5. Let the candle burn safely until you feel a sense of release.

3. Fire Invocation Spell for Passion and Transformation

This spell ignites your inner fire, inspiring creativity and personal transformation.

Ingredients:

- A red or orange candle
- A pinch of cinnamon
- A small piece of paper and pen

Steps:

1. Write your intention or goal on the piece of paper.
2. Light the candle and sprinkle a pinch of cinnamon around it.
3. Say: *"Spirit of Fire, fierce and bright,*
   Ignite my soul with passion's light.
   Transform, renew, and purify,
   With your flames, I soar and fly."
4. Burn the paper in the candle flame (safely) and visualize your intention coming to life.

4. Air Invocation Spell for Clarity and Inspiration

This spell calls upon Air's light and dynamic energy to clear mental fog and spark creativity.

Ingredients:

- A feather or incense stick
- A yellow candle
- A piece of paper and pen

Steps:

1. Light the incense or hold the feather in your hand.

2. Light the yellow candle and say: *"Spirit of Air, swift and free,*
   Bring your clarity and vision to me.
   Clear my mind, inspire my way,
   Let your whispers guide me today."
3. Write down any insights or inspirations that come to you, allowing the element of Air to flow through your thoughts.

Rituals for Weather Control, Fertility, and Purification

Elemental magic also includes rituals to influence the environment, promote growth, and cleanse negative energies.

1. Weather Control Ritual

Use this ritual to summon rain or clear skies, depending on your need.

Ingredients for Rain:

- A bowl of water
- A silver or blue candle
- A shell or pebble from a body of water

Steps:

1. Light the candle and place the water and shell in front of it.
2. Stir the water with your finger and say: *"Waters above, hear my call,*
   Let your tears of rain now fall.
   Life to the Earth, let it be,
   As I will, so mote it be."
3. Pour the water into the soil as an offering.

Ingredients for Clear Skies:

- A yellow candle
- A feather or fan

• A bowl of dry sand

Steps:

1. Light the candle and wave the feather or fan over the sand.
2. Say: *"Winds of change, blow clouds away,*
   Bring the sun to light the day.
   Clear and bright, the skies shall be,
   As I will, so mote it be."

2. Fertility Ritual

This ritual encourages physical or creative fertility, using Earth's nurturing energy.

Ingredients:

• A bowl of fertile soil
• Seeds or a small plant
• A green candle

Steps:

1. Light the green candle and place the soil in front of it.
2. Plant the seeds or small plant in the soil while saying: *"Mother Earth, life you bring,*
   Nurture this seed, let it spring.
   Fertility flows, strong and pure,
   With your blessing, I'm secure."
3. Care for the plant as it grows, symbolizing your fertility or creative success.

3. Purification Ritual

This ritual combines all four elements to cleanse yourself or your space of negativity.

Ingredients:

- Salt (Earth)
- Water (Water)
- A candle (Fire)
- Incense (Air)

Steps:

1. Place the items in a circle, representing the elements.
2. Stand or sit in the center, lighting the candle and incense.
3. Sprinkle salt around yourself and say: *"Earth, ground me."*
4. Sprinkle water around yourself and say: *"Water, cleanse me."*
5. Pass the incense around yourself and say: *"Air, renew me."*
6. Hold your hands near the flame and say: *"Fire, purify me."*
7. Visualize yourself surrounded by radiant, balanced energy.

Charms for Balance and Harmony with Nature

Charms imbued with elemental energy can help you maintain harmony with the natural world.

- **Balance Charm**: Combine a small stone, a feather, a candle wick, and a seashell in a pouch. Carry it to align with all four elements.
- **Harmony Sachet**: Fill a pouch with lavender (Air), rosemary (Earth), cinnamon (Fire), and a drop of water. Place it in your home to create a balanced environment.

Conclusion

Elemental magic is a profound way to connect with the forces of nature and harness their energy for transformation, healing, and growth. By invoking Earth, Water, Fire, and Air, you align yourself with the universe's foundational powers, achieving harmony within yourself and the world around you. As you explore elemental magic, remember to act with respect and gratitude for the natural forces you call upon. Let the elements guide and empower your practice.

Chapter 9: The Spells of the Moon and Stars

The Moon and stars have guided humanity for millennia, their celestial dance shaping the rhythms of life and the tides of magic. The energy of the Moon is transformative, its phases influencing spellwork, intuition, and personal growth. Similarly, the stars and astrological alignments offer guidance, luck, and prosperity, acting as celestial maps for the soul. In this chapter, we explore the potent magic of the Moon and stars, including lunar spells, astrological charms, and rituals for celestial events like eclipses and meteor showers.

Lunar Magic: Harnessing the Moon's Energy

The Moon's phases reflect cycles of growth, release, and renewal, making it a powerful ally in spellwork. Each phase carries unique energy that can be aligned with specific intentions.

The Moon's Phases and Their Magical Uses

1. **New Moon**: A time of new beginnings, intention-setting, and manifestation.
2. **Waxing Crescent**: Growth, attraction, and building energy.
3. **First Quarter**: Taking action, overcoming obstacles, and moving forward.
4. **Waxing Gibbous**: Refinement, preparation, and focus.
5. **Full Moon**: Peak energy, completion, and celebration.
6. **Waning Gibbous**: Gratitude, introspection, and sharing.
7. **Last Quarter**: Release, forgiveness, and letting go.
8. **Waning Crescent**: Rest, reflection, and healing.

Full Moon Spell for Abundance

The Full Moon's energy amplifies intentions, making it ideal for prosperity and abundance spells.

Ingredients:

- A silver or green candle
- A bowl of water
- A coin or small crystal (e.g., citrine or pyrite)

Steps:

1. Place the bowl of water where it can reflect the Full Moon's light (or indoors with a candle).
2. Light the silver or green candle and hold the coin/crystal in your hands.
3. Focus on your intention for abundance and say: *"By the Moon's radiant glow,*
   Prosperity and wealth shall flow.
   Silver light, guide my way,
   Bring abundance, here to stay."
4. Place the coin/crystal in the water to charge it with lunar energy.
5. Keep the coin/crystal as a talisman or bury it in your garden to symbolize growing abundance.

New Moon Spell for Manifestation

The New Moon's energy is perfect for setting intentions and manifesting new opportunities.

Ingredients:

- A piece of paper and pen
- A black or white candle
- A sprig of fresh basil

Steps:

1. Write down your intention or goal on the paper.
2. Light the candle and hold the basil sprig, visualizing your intention coming to life.
3. Say: *"Under the Moon, dark and new,*
   I plant this seed, my dream come true.
   With each day, as light returns,
   My goal ignites, my vision burns."
4. Fold the paper with the basil inside and keep it in a safe place. Revisit it during the Full Moon.

Astrological Charms for Luck, Prosperity, and Guidance

Astrological magic aligns with the energy of the planets, signs, and celestial configurations to create powerful charms.

1. Lucky Star Charm

This charm channels the energy of a favorable astrological alignment for luck and success.

Ingredients:

- A gold or silver star-shaped charm
- A blue or purple ribbon
- Essential oil (e.g., frankincense or sandalwood)

Steps:

1. Anoint the star charm with the essential oil while focusing on your intention for luck.
2. Tie the ribbon to the charm and say: *"Star of fortune, shine so bright,*
   Guide my steps with your light.
   Bring me luck, both day and night,
   Success and joy, my path is right."
3. Wear or carry the charm during important events or opportunities.

2. Prosperity Pouch

This charm combines planetary and zodiac correspondences to attract wealth.

Ingredients:

- A green pouch
- Dried mint and basil
- A coin or small piece of gold
- A written sigil for prosperity

Steps:

1. Fill the pouch with the herbs, coin, and sigil.
2. During a waxing Moon or under a favorable planetary alignment (e.g., Jupiter in Taurus), hold the pouch and say: *"By Jupiter's growth and Venus's grace,*
Prosperity flows, wealth I embrace.
Fortune smiles, abundance grows,
With this charm, success bestows."
3. Keep the pouch in your wallet, purse, or place of business.

Rituals for Celestial Events

Celestial events such as eclipses, meteor showers, and planetary alignments offer unique magical opportunities. These moments of heightened cosmic energy can be harnessed for powerful transformations and insights.

1. Lunar Eclipse Ritual for Release

Lunar eclipses are a time of endings and letting go, ideal for cutting ties with old habits or relationships.

Ingredients:

- A black candle
- A piece of paper and pen
- A fireproof bowl or cauldron

Steps:

1. Write down what you wish to release on the paper.
2. Light the black candle and focus on your intention to let go.
3. Say: *"Shadowed Moon, take my pain,*
   Cleanse my spirit, break this chain.
   Release me now, set me free,
   I embrace my destiny."
4. Burn the paper in the candle flame (safely) and scatter the ashes outdoors.

2. Meteor Shower Wish Ritual

Meteor showers symbolize hope, inspiration, and celestial blessings, making them perfect for wish-making.

Ingredients:

- A small crystal or charm
- A piece of paper and pen

Steps:

1. Write your wish on the paper, keeping it specific and heartfelt.
2. During the meteor shower, hold the crystal/charm and focus on your wish.
3. Say: *"Falling stars, light my way,*
   Carry this wish to realms far away.
   By your spark, my dream shall grow,
   Celestial magic, let it flow."
4. Keep the crystal/charm as a reminder of your wish.

3. Solar Eclipse Spell for Transformation

Solar eclipses signify dramatic change and renewal, ideal for transformative magic.

Ingredients:

- A gold or yellow candle
- A mirror
- A piece of paper and pen

Steps:

1. Write down an area of your life where you seek transformation.
2. Light the candle and place the mirror in front of it.

3. Look into the mirror and say: *"Eclipsed Sun, reveal my light,*
   Transform my path, renew my sight.
   What once was hidden, now I see,
   A stronger, brighter version of me."
4. Burn the paper in the candle flame and bury the ashes outdoors.

Balancing Lunar and Stellar Energies

Working with the Moon and stars creates harmony between your inner and outer worlds. Incorporate both into your practice to align with cosmic rhythms:

- **Daily Guidance**: Use the Moon's phase and astrological transits to guide your spellwork.
- **Personal Zodiac**: Tailor charms and rituals to your Sun, Moon, and Rising signs for personalized magic.
- **Seasonal Magic**: Plan spells around equinoxes, solstices, and other celestial events for maximum potency.

Conclusion

The Moon and stars hold timeless power, offering guidance, transformation, and connection to the greater universe. By working with lunar phases, astrological alignments, and celestial events, you align your magic with the rhythms of the cosmos. Whether invoking the Full Moon's abundance, creating charms under lucky stars, or harnessing the transformative energy of an eclipse, the spells in this chapter help you tap into the infinite magic of the sky. Let the celestial lights inspire your path and illuminate your craft.

Chapter 10: Enchantment and Glamour Spells

Enchantment and glamour spells tap into the art of perception, allowing practitioners to influence how they are seen and experienced by others. From enhancing physical beauty and allure to creating illusions or commanding respect, glamour magic empowers you to shape your image and presence. This form of magic does not alter reality but manipulates the energy and impressions you project, aligning them with your desired outcome.

The Nature of Glamour Magic

Glamour spells are rooted in the principle of energy projection. Your aura, intent, and confidence play key roles in how others perceive you. By amplifying these qualities, you can enhance your natural allure, create illusions, or draw attention.

- **Energy and Intent**: Your personal energy is the foundation of glamour magic. Strong intent amplifies the effectiveness of spells and charms.
- **Self-Belief**: Glamour magic works best when you believe in your desired image or outcome. Confidence is its most potent ingredient.
- **Ethical Considerations**: Glamour spells should never be used to manipulate or deceive maliciously. They are tools for self-expression, empowerment, and confidence.

Spells for Enhancing Physical Beauty and Allure

These spells focus on enhancing your natural features and radiating confidence, helping you present your most magnetic self.

1. Mirror of Beauty Spell

This spell uses a mirror as a magical tool to project beauty and confidence.

Ingredients:

- A hand mirror
- A pink or red candle
- A rose quartz crystal

Steps:

1. Light the candle and place it in front of the mirror. Hold the rose quartz in your hands.
2. Gaze into the mirror, focusing on your reflection. Imagine your aura glowing with warmth and beauty.
3. Say: *"Mirror bright, reflect my light,*
   Let my beauty shine day and night.
   Confidence grows, allure takes flight,
   I radiate charm, pure and right."
4. Carry the rose quartz with you as a talisman of self-love and beauty.

2. Bath of Radiance Ritual

This ritual cleanses your energy and enhances your physical and energetic glow.

Ingredients:

- Rose petals
- Milk or coconut milk
- A few drops of lavender or jasmine essential oil
- A pink or white candle

Steps:

1. Draw a warm bath and add the rose petals, milk, and essential oil.
2. Light the candle and place it near the bath. Step into the water and close your eyes, visualizing yourself bathed in radiant light.
3. Say: *"Water pure, cleanse my soul,*
   Beauty shines, I am whole.
   Glow within, glow without,
   Of my allure, there's no doubt."
4. Soak for 15–20 minutes, focusing on your intention to enhance your radiance.

3. Perfume of Allure

This enchanted perfume enhances your natural charm and attraction.

Ingredients:

- A small bottle of unscented perfume or carrier oil
- A drop each of rose, jasmine, and vanilla essential oils
- A piece of carnelian crystal

Steps:

1. Combine the oils in the perfume bottle and add the carnelian crystal.
2. Hold the bottle and say: *"With this scent, my charm does rise,*
   Beauty glows before all eyes.
   Confidence flows, allure is mine,
   With this magic, I do shine."
3. Apply the perfume to your pulse points before social occasions or important events.

Charms to Create Illusions or Cloak One's Presence

Glamour magic can also be used to create illusions or make yourself less noticeable when desired.

1. Cloak of Shadows Spell

This spell makes you appear inconspicuous or "invisible" to unwanted attention.

Ingredients:

- A black scarf or piece of cloth
- A black candle
- A piece of obsidian or onyx

Steps:

1. Light the black candle and hold the scarf or cloth in your hands.
2. Say: *"Shadows fall, unseen I go,*
   Like the wind, none shall know.
   Cloaked in silence, hidden from sight,
   I move through shadow, veiled by night."
3. Wrap the scarf around your shoulders or carry the cloth with you when you wish to remain unnoticed.

2. Illusion Charm for Mystique

This charm creates an aura of mystery, making others perceive you as intriguing or enigmatic.

Ingredients:

- A piece of amethyst
- A purple ribbon
- A pinch of dried lavender

Steps:

1. Wrap the amethyst in the purple ribbon, tying it securely with the lavender inside.
2. Hold the charm in your hands and say: *"Mystic veil, let my aura grow,*
   Secrets deep, a mystic glow.
   Eyes perceive what I desire,
   Illusion grows, hearts inspire."
3. Carry the charm with you or wear it as a necklace.

Rituals for Commanding Attention and Respect

These rituals help you project authority and magnetism, commanding attention and respect in any situation.

1. The Aura of Command Ritual

This ritual strengthens your presence, making you appear confident and commanding.

Ingredients:

- A gold or yellow candle
- A small mirror
- A piece of citrine or tiger's eye

Steps:

1. Light the candle and place the mirror in front of it.
2. Hold the citrine or tiger's eye and gaze into the mirror, visualizing yourself radiating authority and confidence.
3. Say: *"Sunlight bright, power strong,*
   Respect and trust where I belong.
   My voice is heard, my presence felt,
   With this aura, respect is dealt."
4. Carry the crystal with you during important meetings or events.

2. The Circle of Influence Spell

This spell creates an energetic circle that enhances your ability to influence others.

Ingredients:

- A red or orange candle
- A piece of paper and pen
- A pinch of cinnamon

Steps:

1. Write your name and your desired influence (e.g., "confidence," "respect") on the paper.
2. Light the candle and sprinkle the cinnamon over the paper.
3. Say: *"Circle of power, drawn by flame,*
   Command attention in my name.
   My words are strong, my presence clear,
   Influence grows as all draw near."
4. Burn the paper safely in the candle flame, visualizing your influence expanding outward.

Balancing Glamour and Authenticity

Glamour magic is a tool for enhancing your presence and confidence, but it should always align with your true self. Authenticity amplifies the power of glamour spells, ensuring your projected image resonates with who you are at your core.

- **Self-Care**: Combine glamour magic with self-care practices to enhance both inner and outer beauty.
- **Mindset**: Cultivate positive self-beliefs to reinforce the energy of your glamour spells.
- **Gratitude**: Acknowledge and honor your natural qualities, using glamour magic as an enhancement rather than a mask.

Conclusion

Enchantment and glamour spells empower you to shape your presence and command attention with elegance and confidence. Whether enhancing your natural beauty, creating an aura of mystique, or projecting authority, these spells help you harness the power of perception and energy. Remember that true glamour begins within—embrace your unique qualities and let your magic amplify the light you already possess.

Chapter 11: Voodoo Protection and Warding

Voodoo, with its rich tradition of spirit work and protective magic, offers powerful tools to shield against harm, banish negativity, and establish strong spiritual defenses. This chapter explores spells, rituals, and talismans rooted in Voodoo practices to create protective barriers, summon the guardianship of the Loa (Voodoo spirits), and ensure personal safety through potent amulets.

Understanding Voodoo Protection Magic

Protection is a fundamental aspect of Voodoo, rooted in the belief that spiritual balance and the guidance of the Loa are essential for safeguarding oneself and one's surroundings. Central to Voodoo protection magic are:

- **The Role of the Loa**: These powerful spirits act as intermediaries between humans and the divine, offering guidance, blessings, and protection.
- **Respect for Ancestral and Natural Forces**: Protection rituals often involve connecting with ancestors and the natural elements to establish strong spiritual defenses.
- **Talismans and Symbolism**: Physical objects imbued with spiritual energy, such as veves (sacred symbols), act as protective anchors.

Spells for Creating Protective Barriers Around Property

Establishing a spiritual shield around your home or property is essential for keeping negative energies and harmful entities at bay. The following spells help create a powerful perimeter of protection.

1. Salt and Red Brick Dust Barrier

This spell uses traditional Voodoo materials—salt and red brick dust—to form an impenetrable protective shield.

Ingredients:

- A bowl of salt
- Crushed red brick dust (available at spiritual supply stores or created by grinding a clean red brick)
- A black candle

Steps:

1. Begin by lighting the black candle to symbolize protection and banishment of negativity.
2. Mix the salt and red brick dust in a bowl, focusing on your intention to create a protective barrier.
3. Walk the perimeter of your property, sprinkling the mixture while reciting: *"With salt and dust, this line I draw,*
   A shield of power, without flaw.
   No harm shall pass, no ill may stay,
   My home is safe, night and day."
4. Visualize a shimmering barrier forming as you complete the circle around your property.

2. Veve of Papa Legba for Threshold Protection

Papa Legba, the Loa of crossroads, is a powerful protector of doorways and gateways.

Ingredients:

- Chalk or white flour
- A small offering (such as rum, tobacco, or coins)
- A black or red candle

Steps:

1. Clean the area around your front door or main entryway.
2. Draw Papa Legba's veve (a sacred symbol) on the ground or on paper using chalk or flour. His veve consists of intricate lines, crosses, and loops representing crossroads.
3. Place the candle and offering near the veve. Light the candle and say: *"Papa Legba, guardian true,*
   Protector of paths, I call to you.
   Shield this doorway, keep harm away,
   Your blessings guard both night and day."
4. Leave the offering and veve intact as a spiritual anchor. Redraw the veve periodically to maintain its potency.

Rituals to Summon Loa for Guardianship

Calling upon the Loa for protection requires respect, preparation, and offerings. Below are two rituals to summon specific protective Loa.

1. Ritual to Summon Ogun

Ogun, the Loa of iron, war, and strength, is a powerful guardian against harm and injustice.

Ingredients:

- A small iron tool (e.g., a knife or horseshoe)
- A green or black candle
- A small bowl of rum
- A piece of bread or meat

Steps:

1. Set up an altar with the iron tool, candle, bowl of rum, and offering of bread or meat.
2. Light the candle and hold the iron tool, focusing on your intention to summon Ogun for protection.
3. Say: *"Ogun, warrior bold and true,*
   Protector of steel, I call on you.
   Shield me now, defend my place,
   With your might, danger erase."
4. Pour the rum as a libation and leave the offering on the altar for at least 24 hours.
5. Carry the iron tool with you or place it near your front door as a protective symbol.

2. Ritual to Summon Erzulie Dantor

Erzulie Dantor, the fierce protector of women and children, is invoked for safeguarding loved ones.

Ingredients:

- A blue or pink candle
- A small bowl of Florida Water or rosewater
- A photo or personal item of the person(s) to be protected

Steps:

1. Light the candle and place the bowl of water and photo/personal item on your altar.
2. Say: *"Erzulie Dantor, fierce and wise,*
   Protector of hearts, I seek your ties.
   Guard my loved ones, safe from harm,
   Hold them close within your arm."
3. Dip your fingers in the water and sprinkle it over the photo/item while visualizing protection surrounding the person(s).
4. Keep the photo/item on the altar for ongoing protection.

Talismans and Amulets for Personal Safety

Talismans and amulets are portable items imbued with spiritual energy to protect the wearer from harm and negativity.

1. Gris-Gris Bag for Protection

A gris-gris bag is a traditional Voodoo charm filled with magical ingredients to guard against danger.

Ingredients:

- A small red or black pouch
- Dried herbs (e.g., basil, rosemary, and bay leaves)
- A piece of hematite or obsidian
- A protective sigil or symbol

Steps:

1. Fill the pouch with the herbs, stone, and protective sigil, focusing on your intention to create a powerful charm.
2. Hold the pouch and say: *"By this bag, I am shielded strong,*
   Protected from harm, where I belong.
   Negative forces, you shall not stay,
   I am guarded, night and day."
3. Carry the gris-gris bag with you or place it near your bed for ongoing protection.

2. Protective Amulet of the Crossroads

This amulet connects to the power of crossroads, a sacred space in Voodoo for protection and decision-making.

Ingredients:

- A small metal cross or charm
- A piece of red thread
- A drop of your favorite essential oil (e.g., sandalwood or frankincense)

Steps:

1. Tie the red thread to the cross or charm, imbuing it with your intention for protection.
2. Anoint the charm with the essential oil while saying: *"By the crossroads' power, I stand secure,*
   Guided and guarded, my safety is sure.
   Spirits protect, my path is clear,
   No harm may touch me, far or near."
3. Wear the amulet around your neck or carry it in your pocket.

Maintaining and Reinforcing Protection

- **Periodic Cleansing**: Cleanse your talismans, amulets, and barriers with smoke, salt, or moonlight to maintain their potency.
- **Offerings to the Loa**: Regularly honor the Loa you work with by leaving offerings of their preferred items, such as rum, tobacco, coins, or flowers.
- **Daily Affirmations**: Reinforce your protective magic by repeating affirmations, such as: *"I am protected, strong, and free. Negative energies cannot touch me."*

Conclusion

Voodoo protection and warding offer profound tools for guarding yourself, your loved ones, and your space from harm. By invoking the Loa, crafting potent talismans, and creating spiritual barriers, you can establish a secure and balanced environment. Always approach this work with respect, gratitude, and intention, ensuring the energies you summon align with your highest good. Let the power of Voodoo guide and protect you on your journey.

Chapter 12: Divination Spells

Divination is the art of seeking knowledge and insight through spiritual and mystical means. It has long been a cornerstone of magical practice, helping practitioners uncover hidden truths, foresee potential outcomes, and connect with the spiritual realm. In this chapter, we explore spells for enhancing psychic abilities, charms to communicate with spirits and ancestors, and rituals that incorporate tools like tarot cards, runes, and scrying mirrors.

The Power of Divination

Divination serves as a bridge between the physical and spiritual worlds. By enhancing your intuition and connecting with higher energies, you can gain clarity, wisdom, and guidance. Key principles include:

- **Trusting Your Intuition**: Divination requires an open mind and trust in your inner voice. Developing this trust takes practice but is essential for accuracy.
- **Working with Tools**: Tools like tarot, runes, and scrying mirrors act as focal points for your energy and intention, amplifying your ability to receive messages.
- **Creating a Sacred Space**: A calm and protected environment enhances the clarity and reliability of divination practices.

Spells for Enhancing Psychic Abilities

Psychic abilities such as clairvoyance, dream interpretation, and intuition are the foundation of effective divination. The following spells are designed to strengthen these gifts.

1. Third Eye Activation Spell

This spell enhances your clairvoyance and ability to perceive spiritual insights.

Ingredients:

- A purple candle
- Amethyst crystal
- Lavender essential oil

Steps:

1. Anoint the purple candle with lavender oil and light it in a quiet space.
2. Hold the amethyst crystal to your forehead, over your third eye (the space between your eyebrows).
3. Close your eyes and visualize a glowing indigo light expanding from your third eye.
4. Say: *"Eye of wisdom, open wide,*
   Reveal the truths that here abide.
   Vision clear, insight bright,
   Grant me sight beyond the night."
5. Meditate for 10–15 minutes, focusing on your intention to enhance clairvoyance.

2. Dream Clarity Spell

This spell promotes vivid dreams and strengthens your ability to interpret them.

Ingredients:

- Mugwort or chamomile tea
- A notebook and pen
- A small piece of moonstone

Steps:

1. Brew a cup of mugwort or chamomile tea before bedtime to relax and enhance dream recall.
2. Hold the moonstone and say: *"Dreams of wisdom, vivid and clear,*
   Guide my spirit, let truth appear.
   As I sleep, my mind shall see,
   Visions of what is meant to be."
3. Place the moonstone under your pillow and keep the notebook and pen nearby to record your dreams upon waking.

Charms for Communicating with Spirits and Ancestors

Communication with spirits and ancestors requires focus, respect, and intention. These charms help establish and maintain a strong connection.

1. Ancestral Connection Charm

This charm strengthens your bond with ancestral spirits, aiding in guidance and protection.

Ingredients:

- A white pouch
- Dried rosemary and bay leaves
- A small piece of quartz
- A photo or small item connected to your ancestors

Steps:

1. Fill the pouch with the dried herbs and quartz.
2. Hold the pouch and photo/item in your hands and say: *"Ancestors wise, hear my plea,*
   Guide and protect, walk with me.
   Through this charm, our bond is strong,
   Your wisdom guides me all day long."
3. Keep the charm on your altar or carry it with you during divination sessions.

2. Spirit Communication Pendant

This pendant facilitates safe and clear communication with spirits.

Ingredients:

- A silver or black pendant
- A strand of your hair or a personal item
- A piece of hematite or obsidian

Steps:

1. Attach the personal item to the pendant to link it to your energy.
2. Hold the pendant and hematite while saying: *"Spirit voices, clear and true,*
   Through this charm, I call to you.
   With respect and love, I seek your guide,
   Protect me always, by my side."
3. Wear the pendant during spirit communication rituals for enhanced clarity and protection.

Rituals Using Tarot, Runes, and Scrying Mirrors

Divination tools serve as gateways to deeper understanding. These rituals incorporate tarot cards, runes, and scrying mirrors for specific purposes.

1. Tarot Spell for Decision-Making

This ritual uses tarot cards to gain clarity and guidance when faced with a difficult decision.

Ingredients:

- A tarot deck
- A candle (white for clarity, yellow for insight)
- A small bowl of water

Steps:

1. Light the candle and place the bowl of water nearby to create a calm atmosphere.
2. Shuffle the tarot deck while focusing on your question or decision.
3. Draw three cards, representing:
    ◦ The past (what led to the situation)
    ◦ The present (current influences)
    ◦ The future (potential outcomes)
4. Lay the cards in front of you and interpret their meanings. Write down your impressions and reflect on the guidance they provide.

2. Rune Casting for Guidance

Runes are ancient symbols used for insight and wisdom. This ritual aids in uncovering hidden truths.

Ingredients:

- A set of runes
- A piece of cloth or small mat
- A question or area of focus

Steps:

1. Spread the cloth or mat in front of you to define your casting area.
2. Hold the runes in your hands, focusing on your question or intention.
3. Scatter the runes onto the cloth and observe which symbols land face-up.
4. Interpret the meanings of the runes and their positions relative to each other, noting patterns or significant messages.

3. Scrying Mirror Ritual for Vision

A scrying mirror is a powerful tool for accessing visions and spiritual insights.

Ingredients:

- A black scrying mirror or dark bowl filled with water
- A candle (silver or blue)
- Incense (e.g., mugwort or sandalwood)

Steps:

1. Light the candle and incense, placing them near the scrying mirror or bowl.
2. Sit comfortably and gaze into the reflective surface, allowing your mind to relax.
3. Say: *"Portal of shadow, clear and deep,*
   Show me visions, truths to keep.
   Through the veil, I seek to see,
   Wisdom, clarity, come to me."
4. Observe any images, symbols, or impressions that appear. Write them down immediately after the ritual to analyze later.

Cleansing and Protection in Divination

Working with spirits and divination tools requires spiritual hygiene to maintain clarity and safety. Incorporate these practices:

- **Cleanse Tools Regularly**: Use smoke (sage, palo santo) or moonlight to cleanse tarot cards, runes, or scrying mirrors.
- **Circle of Protection**: Before divination, cast a protective circle to prevent interference from unwanted energies.
- **Grounding and Centering**: After divination, ground your energy by touching the Earth, eating, or holding grounding stones like hematite or obsidian.

Conclusion

Divination spells and rituals open the door to profound insights and spiritual connections, empowering you to navigate life's mysteries with wisdom and clarity. By enhancing your psychic abilities, communicating with spirits and ancestors, and mastering tools like tarot, runes, and scrying mirrors, you align yourself with the flow of universal knowledge. Approach this work with respect, patience, and intention, and the secrets of the unseen will reveal themselves to you.

Chapter 13: Binding and Banishing Spells

Binding and banishing are essential practices in magical traditions, designed to neutralize threats, dispel negativity, and establish spiritual safety. Binding spells restrict the influence of harmful people or spirits, while banishing rituals cleanse spaces of malevolent energies or entities. Combined with protection charms, these practices create a fortress of spiritual defense, ensuring your energy and environment remain harmonious.

Understanding Binding and Banishing

Before performing binding or banishing spells, it's important to understand their ethical and spiritual implications:

- **Binding**: This act restricts someone or something's ability to cause harm. It doesn't aim to harm them but to neutralize their negative influence.
- **Banishing**: This removes unwanted energies, entities, or influences from a person or space. Banishing is often followed by protection to prevent reentry.
- **Respect for Free Will**: Use binding and banishing responsibly, ensuring your intentions are justifiable and align with the greater good.

Spells for Binding Enemies or Harmful Spirits

Binding spells create energetic restraints, preventing harm while containing the target's negative influence.

1. Cord Binding Spell

This spell binds an enemy or harmful influence, rendering them powerless to act against you.

Ingredients:

- A black cord or piece of string
- A small piece of paper and pen
- A black candle

Steps:

1. Write the name of the person or entity you wish to bind on the piece of paper. Fold the paper three times.
2. Light the black candle and focus on your intention to neutralize their influence.
3. Wrap the cord tightly around the folded paper, tying it securely as you say: *"Bound by cord, your harm shall cease,*
   From this day forth, I claim my peace.
   Your power ends, your hold is done,
   My will is strong, this spell is spun."
4. Store the bound paper in a safe, hidden place. When you feel the binding is no longer necessary, burn or bury the cord and paper to release the energy.

2. Mirror Binding for Reflection

This binding spell uses a mirror to reflect negativity back to its source.

Ingredients:

- A small mirror
- A black cloth
- A piece of paper and pen

Steps:

1. Write the name of the harmful person or spirit on the piece of paper.
2. Place the paper face-down on the mirror and wrap them together in the black cloth.
3. Hold the wrapped mirror and say: *"Mirror bright, reflect their spite,*
   Contain their harm, hold them tight.
   What they send, shall now return,
   Their power fades, their lessons learn."
4. Store the wrapped mirror in a dark, undisturbed place.

Banishing Rituals to Rid Spaces of Negative Energy

Banishing rituals cleanse spaces of negative energies, harmful entities, and lingering emotional residue.

1. Salt and Smoke Banishing Ritual

This classic banishing ritual combines the cleansing power of salt and smoke to purify a space.

Ingredients:

- A bowl of salt
- A bundle of sage, palo santo, or incense
- A bell or chime (optional)

Steps:

1. Begin at the main entrance of your space, lighting the sage or incense to produce cleansing smoke.
2. Sprinkle a small amount of salt across doorways, windowsills, and corners as you move through each room.
3. As you work, say: *"Negative energy, you cannot stay,*
   I cleanse this space; be gone this day.
   By salt and smoke, this home is free,
   Only light and love may dwell with me."
4. Ring the bell or chime in each room to break up stagnant energy.
5. Once complete, dispose of any ashes or leftover salt outside, away from your home.

2. Circle of Light Banishing Ritual

This ritual uses visualization and candle magic to banish negativity.

Ingredients:

- A white candle
- A small bowl of water
- A piece of clear quartz

Steps:

1. Light the white candle in the center of the space you wish to cleanse.
2. Hold the quartz in your hands and focus on your intention to banish negativity.
3. Walk clockwise around the room, sprinkling the water and visualizing a circle of radiant light expanding outward.
4. Say: *"Light of purity, light of grace,*
   Remove all darkness from this place.
   By fire, water, and spirit's might,
   I banish shadows, restore the light."
5. Place the quartz near the candle to absorb any lingering negativity.

Protection Charms for Warding Off Curses and Hexes

Protection charms create ongoing spiritual defenses, shielding you from harm and malicious magic.

1. Witch's Bottle for Protection

A witch's bottle acts as a protective talisman, capturing and neutralizing harmful energy.

Ingredients:

- A small glass jar with a lid
- Sharp objects (e.g., nails, pins, or broken glass)
- Salt and vinegar
- A small piece of your hair or nail clippings

Steps:

1. Fill the jar with the sharp objects, symbolizing a barrier against harm.
2. Add salt and vinegar to the jar, visualizing the neutralization of negative energy.
3. Place your hair or nail clippings inside to link the protection to you.
4. Seal the jar and say: *"Bottle strong, my shield you'll be,*
   Guard my spirit, protect me free.
   Harm directed, here shall stay,
   Captured within, it fades away."
5. Bury the jar near your home's entrance or keep it in a hidden, secure location.

2. Protection Amulet

This simple charm is carried or worn to ward off curses and hexes.

Ingredients:

- A small pouch
- Dried rosemary and thyme
- A piece of black tourmaline or obsidian

Steps:

1. Fill the pouch with the herbs and stone, focusing on your intention for protection.
2. Hold the pouch and say: *"Herbs and stone, my shield you'll be,*
   Warding harm and negativity.
   By your power, curses break,
   My safety grows, no ill can take."
3. Carry the pouch with you or hang it near your bed for ongoing protection.

3. Sigil of Warding

A sigil is a powerful symbol imbued with protective energy.

Steps to Create and Activate a Sigil:

1. Write down your intention, such as "I am protected from harm."
2. Remove repeating letters to form a unique sequence.
3. Rearrange the remaining letters into an abstract design or symbol.
4. Draw the sigil on paper or carve it into a candle, focusing on your intent.
5. Charge the sigil by meditating on it or burning the candle, saying:
   "Sigil strong, your power grows,
   Shield me now, as the energy flows.

Harm is stopped, protection near,
My ward is strong, I have no fear."

6. Keep the sigil in your home, on your person, or redraw it periodically for reinforcement.

Maintaining Protection and Cleansing

After performing binding or banishing spells, maintain your defenses to prevent the return of negative energies:

- **Regular Cleansing**: Cleanse your home and personal energy weekly using smoke, salt, or moonlight.
- **Gratitude Offerings**: Thank any spirits or deities you worked with, leaving offerings such as incense, water, or flowers.
- **Check Protective Charms**: Inspect and recharge your charms and talismans as needed to keep their energy strong.

Conclusion

Binding and banishing are powerful forms of magical protection, ensuring your personal space and energy remain free from harm. By combining spells, rituals, and charms, you can neutralize threats, cleanse negativity, and establish a fortified spiritual boundary. Approach this work with respect, clarity, and intention, and you will wield the strength to safeguard yourself and those you love. Let your magic be a shield, empowering you to live with confidence and peace.

Chapter 14: Wealth and Prosperity Magic

Wealth and prosperity magic is rooted in aligning your energy with the abundant forces of the universe. Through focused intention, symbolism, and spiritual practices, you can attract financial opportunities, foster business success, and overcome obstacles to abundance. This chapter explores spells, charms, and rituals designed to draw money, success, and growth into your life while breaking through limiting financial blockages.

Understanding Prosperity Magic

Prosperity magic is more than just attracting money; it's about creating a flow of abundance in every aspect of your life. This requires:

1. **Clear Intentions**: Define what prosperity means to you—financial gain, career success, or opportunities for growth.
2. **Alignment with Energy**: Cultivate a mindset of gratitude and confidence to align your energy with abundance.
3. **Consistency in Practice**: Regularly perform spells and rituals to maintain a strong connection with prosperity energies.

Spells for Attracting Money, Success, and Opportunities

These spells are designed to invite wealth and success into your life by harnessing symbols of prosperity and focusing your intentions.

1. Money Magnet Spell

This spell amplifies your ability to attract financial opportunities and wealth.

Ingredients:

- A green candle
- A small magnet
- A dollar bill or coin
- Basil and cinnamon (dried)

Steps:

1. Place the magnet on your altar or workspace. Surround it with the basil, cinnamon, and the dollar bill/coin.
2. Light the green candle and focus on your intention to attract money and opportunities.
3. Say: *"Money flows, like a stream so wide,*
   Opportunities come, by my side.
   Wealth and fortune, here to stay,
   Abundance grows, day by day."
4. Keep the magnet in your wallet or place it where you manage finances to draw wealth.

2. Golden Opportunity Spell

This spell helps open doors to career and business opportunities.

Ingredients:

- A gold candle
- A pinch of allspice or nutmeg
- A piece of citrine or tiger's eye

Steps:

1. Light the gold candle and sprinkle the allspice around it.
2. Hold the citrine or tiger's eye in your hand and visualize opportunities flowing toward you.
3. Say: *"Golden flame, bright and true,
   Open doors, let success shine through.
   Opportunities, come to me,
   My path is clear, as it's meant to be."*
4. Keep the stone with you during job interviews, meetings, or decision-making processes.

3. Abundance Jar Spell

Create a jar filled with symbols of prosperity to continually attract wealth.

Ingredients:

- A small glass jar
- Coins and a dollar bill
- Dried mint, basil, and bay leaves
- A piece of green or gold ribbon

Steps:

1. Fill the jar with the coins, dollar bill, and herbs, layering them to represent growing abundance.
2. Seal the jar and tie the ribbon around it while saying: *"Fortune grows, like seeds in the earth,*
   Abundance flows, wealth and worth.
   By this jar, my wealth expands,
   Prosperity flows, as I command."
3. Place the jar on your desk, altar, or a safe space where you manage money.

Charms for Business Growth and Abundance

Charms are portable and powerful tools to maintain a constant flow of success and prosperity energy.

1. Prosperity Coin Charm

Carry this charm to attract financial growth and business success.

Ingredients:

- A shiny coin
- A pinch of dried mint
- A green pouch or cloth

Steps:

1. Wrap the coin in the cloth or place it in the pouch along with the mint.
2. Hold the charm in your hands and say: *"Coin of wealth, mint of gain,*
   Bring success, remove all strain.
   Prosperity grows where I may go,
   Abundance follows, as I know."
3. Carry the charm in your pocket or wallet.

2. Business Success Talisman

This talisman enhances the growth and success of your business.

Ingredients:

- A small figurine or symbol representing your business (e.g., a key for opening doors, a feather for inspiration)
- A gold thread
- A small crystal (citrine or pyrite)

Steps:

1. Wrap the figurine or symbol with the gold thread, tying the crystal to it.
2. Hold the talisman and visualize your business flourishing, with customers, clients, and opportunities flowing to you.
3. Say: *"Success is mine, my business thrives,*
   Prosperity grows, dreams come alive.
   By this charm, fortune's door,
   Opens wide, and profits soar."
4. Place the talisman on your work desk or in your business space.

Rituals to Break Through Financial Blockages

Financial blockages often stem from limiting beliefs or negative energy surrounding money. These rituals help clear those obstacles.

1. Cord Cutting Ritual for Financial Freedom

This ritual severs ties with negative financial habits or past struggles.

Ingredients:

- A black candle
- A piece of cord or string
- A piece of paper and pen

Steps:

1. Write down financial habits or situations you wish to release on the paper.
2. Tie a knot in the cord to represent the blockages.
3. Light the black candle and hold the cord over the flame (safely, without burning yourself) as you say: *"Bound no more by the past I see,*
   Financial chains, I set you free.
   Prosperity flows, clear and true,
   A path of wealth I now pursue."
4. Cut the cord and burn the paper in the candle flame, releasing the blockages.

2. Flow of Wealth Cleansing Ritual

This ritual clears stagnant energy and encourages financial growth.

Ingredients:

- A bowl of water
- Sea salt
- A sprig of fresh rosemary

Steps:

1. Add sea salt to the bowl of water and stir with the rosemary sprig.
2. Walk through your space, sprinkling the water lightly as you say:
   "Flow of wealth, unblocked and free,
   Abundance flows, come to me.
   Stagnant energy, now released,
   Financial blessings are increased."
3. Dispose of the remaining water outside to symbolically release negativity.

3. Moonlight Wealth Renewal Ritual

Perform this ritual during a new moon to reset your financial energy and attract fresh opportunities.

Ingredients:

- A silver or green candle
- A piece of paper and pen
- A bowl of water

Steps:

1. Write down your financial goals and place the paper under the bowl of water.
2. Light the candle and position it near the bowl, allowing its reflection to shine in the water.
3. Say: *"Under this moon, new and bright,
   I call abundance into my sight.
   Money flows, success takes root,
   Prosperity grows, from seed to fruit."*
4. Leave the bowl and candle on your altar overnight. The next day, pour the water into the Earth as an offering.

Maintaining Wealth and Prosperity Magic

- **Gratitude Practice**: Regularly express gratitude for your current wealth, no matter how small. Gratitude aligns your energy with abundance.
- **Consistent Cleansing**: Clear stagnant financial energy by performing cleansing rituals monthly.
- **Recharging Charms**: Periodically cleanse and recharge your charms under the light of the full moon or by placing them in a bed of salt.

Conclusion

Wealth and prosperity magic empowers you to attract financial opportunities, overcome blockages, and create a flow of abundance in your life. By aligning your energy, using spells and charms, and performing rituals with intention, you can transform your financial reality. Remember that prosperity begins within; cultivate a mindset of abundance, gratitude, and confidence, and watch as the universe responds in kind. Let your magic be the key that unlocks the doors to your success.

Chapter 15: Voodoo Love and Relationship Spells

Love is one of the most profound forces that magic seeks to influence, and in the Voodoo tradition, love spells are imbued with spiritual depth and vibrant energy. Through rituals invoking the Loa, spells for rekindling passion, and practices to strengthen emotional bonds, Voodoo love magic connects practitioners with the spiritual realm to bring harmony, passion, and fulfillment to relationships. This chapter also explores the ethical considerations of love magic, emphasizing the importance of consent and respect.

The Power of Love Magic in Voodoo

Love magic in Voodoo is deeply intertwined with respect for the Loa, spirits who guide and influence human affairs. When working with the Loa, practitioners offer gifts and seek their blessings to achieve love, strengthen relationships, or encourage fertility. Key principles include:

1. **Working with the Loa**: Specific Loa, such as Erzulie Freda (love and beauty) or Damballa (fertility and creation), are often invoked in love rituals.
2. **Energy of Intent**: Love magic amplifies your intentions and desires, so clarity and sincerity are essential.
3. **Ethical Boundaries**: Respect for free will and mutual consent is paramount in love magic to avoid unintended karmic consequences.

Rituals Invoking Loa for Love, Marriage, and Fertility

The Loa are powerful allies in love magic. These rituals call upon their guidance and blessings for specific relationship goals.

1. Erzulie Freda Ritual for Love and Beauty

Erzulie Freda, the Loa of love, beauty, and luxury, is a compassionate spirit who helps attract and maintain love.

Ingredients:

- A pink or red candle
- A bowl of rose petals
- A bottle of perfume or scented oil
- Offerings (e.g., jewelry, sweets, or rum)

Steps:

1. Create an altar with the candle, rose petals, perfume, and offerings. Arrange the items beautifully to honor Erzulie Freda.
2. Light the candle and say: *"Erzulie Freda, spirit of love,*
   Hear my plea from realms above.
   Bless my heart, let love abound,
   Beauty and passion all around."
3. Anoint yourself with the perfume or scented oil, visualizing love flowing into your life.
4. Leave the offerings on the altar overnight as a gesture of gratitude.

2. Damballa Ritual for Fertility and Creation

Damballa, the serpent Loa, represents life, fertility, and creation. This ritual seeks his blessings for conception or creative projects.

Ingredients:

- A white candle
- A bowl of water
- A white cloth
- Offerings (e.g., eggs, white flowers, or milk)

Steps:

1. Set up an altar with the candle, bowl of water, white cloth, and offerings.
2. Light the candle and dip your hands into the water, sprinkling it over the cloth as a sign of purification.
3. Say: *"Damballa, serpent pure and wise,*
   Bless this union under the skies.
   Life and creation, strong and true,
   Bring forth blessings in all we do."
4. Leave the offerings on the altar for 24 hours, then dispose of them respectfully in nature.

3. Marriage Blessing Ritual

This ritual strengthens the bond between partners, promoting harmony and long-term commitment.

Ingredients:

- Two white candles
- A piece of white string or ribbon
- A bowl of honey

Steps:

1. Place the two candles side by side and tie them together with the string or ribbon to symbolize union.
2. Light the candles and say: *"Spirits of love, spirits of peace,*
   Bless this union, let joy increase.
   Hearts entwined, forever strong,
   Love eternal, where we belong."
3. Dip your fingers in the honey and feed each other a small taste to symbolize sweetness in your relationship.
4. Let the candles burn down safely, keeping the string or ribbon as a token of your bond.

Spells for Rekindling Passion or Strengthening Bonds

Love, like any relationship, requires nurturing. These spells help reignite passion or deepen emotional connections.

1. Passion Flame Spell

This spell reignites passion and intimacy between partners.

Ingredients:

- A red candle
- A cinnamon stick
- A photo or object representing both partners

Steps:

1. Light the red candle and place the photo or object in front of it.
2. Hold the cinnamon stick and say: *"Flame of passion, strong and bright,*
   Rekindle love in the softest light.
   Desire grows, connection renews,
   Hearts aligned, our love imbues."
3. Pass the cinnamon stick through the flame (safely) and place it near your bed to inspire intimacy.

2. Bond-Strengthening Charm

This charm reinforces trust and communication between partners.

Ingredients:

- A piece of blue cloth
- Dried lavender and rose petals
- A small crystal (e.g., rose quartz or clear quartz)

Steps:

1. Place the lavender, rose petals, and crystal in the center of the blue cloth.
2. Tie the cloth into a pouch and say: *"By this charm, our bond is sealed,*
   Stronger with time, our hearts revealed.
   Trust and love, deep and true,
   Together as one, me and you."
3. Place the charm in your bedroom or a shared space to maintain its energy.

Warnings and Ethical Considerations for Love Spells

Love spells hold great power and responsibility. Misusing this magic can lead to unintended consequences for all involved. Follow these guidelines to ensure ethical practice:

1. Respect Free Will

- Never use love magic to force someone to feel something against their will. True love cannot be coerced, and spells that attempt to manipulate emotions can lead to karmic repercussions.

2. Focus on Self-Love

- Before casting love spells for others, ensure your self-love and confidence are strong. A foundation of self-worth enhances the effectiveness of your magic and attracts healthier relationships.

3. Consider Long-Term Consequences

- Reflect on whether the spell aligns with your true desires and values. Spells that bind or manipulate may lead to regret or complications in the future.

4. Use Protection

- When working with the Loa or performing powerful love spells, always create a protective space by casting a circle or invoking guardian spirits to ensure your safety and well-being.

Conclusion

Voodoo love and relationship spells connect you to the profound energies of the Loa and the power of your own intentions. Whether seeking love, rekindling passion, or strengthening bonds, these practices foster connection and harmony when used responsibly and respectfully. By aligning your energy with compassion and mutual respect, you create space for love to flourish authentically. Let your love magic be a beacon of light, drawing beauty and fulfillment into your relationships.

Chapter 16: Dream and Sleep Spells

Dreams are a gateway to the subconscious mind and the spiritual realm, offering profound insights, healing, and mystical experiences. Dream and sleep spells tap into the energy of the dream world to promote restful sleep, protect against nightmares, enable lucid dreaming, and harness the power of dreams for prophetic visions. In this chapter, we explore charms, spells, and rituals to enhance your dream magic and deepen your connection to the mysteries of sleep.

The Magic of Dreams

Dreams have long been revered as sacred messages from the divine or the subconscious. The practice of dream magic emphasizes:

1. **Lucid Dreaming**: The ability to consciously navigate and manipulate your dreams.
2. **Astral Travel**: Journeying beyond the physical body into spiritual or astral realms.
3. **Prophetic Dreams**: Receiving messages, guidance, or warnings through dream symbolism.
4. **Protective Sleep**: Ensuring a safe and restful sleep environment to support spiritual work.

Charms for Lucid Dreaming and Astral Travel

Lucid dreaming and astral travel require focused intention and energetic preparation. These charms help you achieve clarity and control in the dream realm.

1. Lucid Dreaming Pillow Sachet

This charm enhances your ability to recognize and control your dreams.

Ingredients:

- A small cloth pouch
- Dried mugwort and lavender
- A piece of clear quartz or amethyst

Steps:

1. Fill the pouch with mugwort, lavender, and the crystal.
2. Hold the pouch in your hands and say: *"Dreams of clarity, visions bright,*
   Guide my soul through the night.
   Awareness grows, I take control,
   Lucid dreams shall be my goal."
3. Place the sachet under your pillow to promote lucid dreaming.

2. Astral Travel Talisman

This talisman aids in safe and guided astral projection during sleep.

Ingredients:

- A silver charm or pendant
- A blue ribbon
- A drop of sandalwood oil

Steps:

1. Anoint the charm with the sandalwood oil, focusing on your intention for safe and insightful astral travel.
2. Tie the blue ribbon to the charm and say: *"Bound by silver, safe and free,*
   My spirit soars, where it's meant to be.
   Through astral realms, I journey wide,
   Guided and safe, with spirits by my side."
3. Wear the talisman or place it under your pillow before sleep.

Spells for Warding Off Nightmares and Sleep Disturbances

Protection during sleep ensures your mind and body are safe from harmful energies, negative dreams, or restless nights.

1. Nightmares Banishing Spell

This spell creates a barrier of protection around your sleeping space.

Ingredients:

- A black or white candle
- A pinch of salt
- A piece of obsidian or black tourmaline

Steps:

1. Light the candle and sprinkle salt around your bed in a clockwise circle.
2. Hold the obsidian or black tourmaline and say: *"Darkest dreams, you have no place,*
   Leave this room, leave this space.
   Peaceful rest is all I keep,
   Within this circle, safely I sleep."
3. Place the crystal under your pillow or beside your bed for ongoing protection.

2. Dreamcatcher Cleansing Ritual

Enhance the protective energy of a dreamcatcher to ward off nightmares.

Ingredients:

- A dreamcatcher
- Sage or palo santo for smudging
- A bowl of water with a pinch of salt

Steps:

1. Smudge the dreamcatcher with sage or palo santo to cleanse it of negative energy.
2. Dip your fingers in the salted water and sprinkle it over the dreamcatcher while saying: *"Sacred web, catch what's foul,*
   Let no harm pass, nor spirits prowl.
   Peaceful sleep, my dreams are clear,
   Only light and love may linger near."
3. Hang the dreamcatcher above your bed for continued protection.

Rituals to Harness the Power of Dreams for Prophecy

Prophetic dreams provide guidance and insight into future events or hidden truths. These rituals enhance your ability to receive and interpret dream messages.

1. Moonlight Dream Prophecy Ritual

This ritual channels lunar energy to enhance prophetic dreams.

Ingredients:

- A silver or white candle
- A piece of paper and pen
- A bowl of water
- A moonstone crystal

Steps:

1. Light the silver or white candle and place the bowl of water nearby.
2. Write your question or area of concern on the paper.
3. Hold the moonstone over the water and say: *"Moonlight bright, guide my sight,*
   Dreams reveal what's hidden in night.
   By lunar glow, truth shall flow,
   Answers clear, to me they'll show."
4. Place the paper under your pillow and sleep with the moonstone nearby. Record any dreams upon waking.

2. Herb-Infused Dream Tea Ritual

This ritual uses herbs to induce vivid dreams and enhance intuition.
Ingredients:

- A tea blend of mugwort, chamomile, and peppermint
- Honey (optional)

Steps:

1. Brew the tea before bedtime, focusing on your intention for dream prophecy.
2. As you sip the tea, say: *"Herbal brew, visions flow,*
   Secrets of the night, let me know.
   Dreams of truth, dreams divine,
   Guide me to what's truly mine."
3. Keep a journal by your bed to record any significant dreams.

Interpreting and Honoring Dream Messages

To fully harness the power of dreams, it's essential to understand their messages and symbols. Follow these steps:

1. **Keep a Dream Journal**: Write down your dreams immediately upon waking, capturing as many details as possible.
2. **Look for Patterns**: Pay attention to recurring symbols, themes, or emotions in your dreams.
3. **Use Divination Tools**: Incorporate tarot, runes, or pendulums to clarify dream meanings.
4. **Honor the Guidance**: Act on the insights or warnings received in your dreams to show respect for their messages.

Maintaining a Sacred Sleep Space

To support your dream work and ensure restful sleep, create a sacred environment:

- **Cleanse Regularly**: Smudge your bedroom with sage or palo santo to remove stagnant energy.
- **Add Crystals**: Use amethyst, moonstone, or selenite to enhance dream clarity and spiritual connection.
- **Set Intentions**: Before sleep, set a clear intention for your dreams, such as seeking guidance, clarity, or healing.

Conclusion

Dream and sleep spells unlock the mysteries of the dream realm, enabling you to access deeper insights, healing, and spiritual experiences. Whether enhancing lucid dreaming, protecting against nightmares, or seeking prophetic visions, these practices strengthen your connection to the dream world and the wisdom it holds. By combining magical preparation with an open mind, you can turn your dreams into a powerful tool for transformation and growth. Let the magic of the night guide your spirit and illuminate your path.

Chapter 17: Death and Afterlife Spells

Death, the ultimate mystery, has been a focus of magical practices for centuries. In many traditions, including necromancy, the veil between the living and the dead is a space for connection, guidance, and resolution. This chapter explores rituals for communicating with the dead, guiding spirits to the afterlife, and creating protective charms for dealing with restless souls. While death magic holds immense power, it requires great respect, care, and preparation to ensure safety and balance.

Understanding Death Magic

Death magic is not about defying mortality but working with the energies of transition, memory, and spirit. Practitioners of this magic understand the following principles:

1. **Respect for the Dead**: Spirits should always be approached with reverence and clear intentions. Misusing death magic can lead to unintended consequences.
2. **The Role of the Practitioner**: You serve as a bridge between realms, facilitating communication, healing, or resolution for both the living and the dead.
3. **Spiritual Protection**: Working with death energy requires strong protective measures to guard against malevolent entities or spiritual attachments.

Necromancy Rituals for Communicating with the Dead

Necromancy involves contacting spirits to seek guidance, uncover hidden truths, or resolve unfinished business. The following rituals facilitate respectful and safe communication.

1. Ancestor Contact Ritual

This ritual connects you with benevolent ancestors for wisdom and protection.

Ingredients:

- A white candle
- A photograph or object connected to the ancestor
- A bowl of water
- A pinch of salt

Steps:

1. Create an altar with the candle, photograph/object, and bowl of water. Sprinkle salt into the water to purify it.
2. Light the candle and say: *"Ancestors wise, hear my plea,*
   Come forth now and speak to me.
   With love and respect, I seek your guide,
   Protect my path and stand by my side."
3. Focus on the photograph or object and pay attention to impressions, thoughts, or sensations that arise. Write down any messages you receive.
4. When finished, thank the ancestor and extinguish the candle.

2. Graveyard Necromancy Ritual

This advanced ritual is performed in a graveyard to communicate with a specific spirit.

Ingredients:

- A black candle
- An offering (e.g., flowers, coins, or bread)
- A pendulum or scrying mirror

Steps:

1. Find a quiet and respectful spot in the graveyard near the grave of the spirit you wish to contact.
2. Light the black candle and place the offering on the grave.
3. Say: *"Spirit resting, I call to thee,*
   If willing, come and speak with me.
   I seek your wisdom, guidance, or aid,
   With respect, this request is made."
4. Use the pendulum or scrying mirror to receive answers or impressions. If using a pendulum, ask yes/no questions; if scrying, observe the mirror for symbols or visions.
5. Thank the spirit and leave the offering behind as a token of gratitude.

Spells for Guiding Spirits to the Afterlife

Sometimes spirits become trapped or restless, unable to move on. These spells help guide them to the afterlife with compassion and respect.

1. Crossing Over Ritual

This ritual gently assists a restless spirit in transitioning to the afterlife.

Ingredients:

- A white candle
- A bell or chime
- A bundle of sage or palo santo

Steps:

1. Light the white candle and cleanse the space with sage or palo santo.
2. Ring the bell or chime three times to call the spirit's attention.
3. Say: *"Spirit wandering, find your peace,*
   From this realm, I grant release.
   Follow the light, where love does glow,
   To the place where you must go."
4. Visualize a bright, warm light enveloping the spirit and leading them upward. Hold this visualization until you feel the energy shift.
5. Thank the spirit for their presence and extinguish the candle.

2. Water Offering for the Departed

This spell uses water as a medium to cleanse and release lingering spirits.

Ingredients:

- A bowl of clean water
- A white flower (e.g., a lily or daisy)
- A pinch of sea salt

Steps:

1. Place the bowl of water on your altar or in the area where you sense the restless spirit.
2. Add the sea salt and float the flower on the water's surface.
3. Say: *"Spirit pure, bound no more,*
   By water's flow, cross through the door.
   Peace be yours, rest be true,
   Your journey ends; we honor you."
4. Dispose of the water and flower in a natural body of water or the Earth as a final offering.

Protective Charms for Dealing with Restless Souls

Working with death magic requires strong spiritual protections to guard against harmful or mischievous spirits.

1. Spirit Warding Amulet

This charm protects you from restless or malevolent spirits.

Ingredients:

- A black cord or ribbon
- A piece of obsidian or hematite
- Dried rosemary and salt

Steps:

1. Tie the obsidian or hematite to the black cord, incorporating the rosemary and a pinch of salt into the knot.
2. Hold the charm and say: *"Stone of shadow, herbs of might,*
   Protect my soul, both day and night.
   Wards I raise, no harm shall near,
   I stand secure, free from fear."
3. Wear the amulet or keep it on your person during death magic rituals.

2. Protective Salt Circle

This spell creates a sacred, protected space for working with spirits.

Ingredients:

- Sea salt
- A small bowl of water
- A white candle

Steps:

1. Light the candle and sprinkle sea salt in a circle around your working area.
2. Dip your fingers in the bowl of water and anoint the edges of the salt circle.
3. Say: *"Sacred circle, strong and sure,*
   No spirit crosses, impure.
   Within this space, my will is law,
   Protected by light, without a flaw."
4. Perform your ritual within the circle, extinguishing the candle when finished.

Ethical Considerations in Death Magic

Death magic carries significant spiritual responsibility. Always follow these ethical guidelines:

1. **Consent and Respect**: Never summon or disturb spirits against their will.
2. **Honoring the Dead**: Treat spirits and graveyards with reverence, leaving offerings and showing gratitude.
3. **Spiritual Cleansing**: After working with death energy, cleanse yourself and your space to release lingering energies.

Conclusion

Death and afterlife spells connect you to the mysteries of the spiritual realm, offering opportunities for healing, guidance, and resolution. By practicing necromancy rituals, guiding restless spirits, and using protective charms, you honor the transition between life and death while maintaining safety and balance. Approach this work with respect, intention, and care, and the magic of the afterlife will reveal its profound wisdom and power.

Chapter 18: Curses and Hexes of the White Witch

Curses and hexes are among the most potent and controversial forms of magic, wielded as tools of retribution or justice when all other means have failed. While they can deliver swift and powerful results, they also carry significant ethical, karmic, and spiritual risks. In this chapter, we explore advanced spells for hexing, methods for breaking or reversing curses, and the profound consequences of working with dark magic.

Understanding the Nature of Curses and Hexes

A curse or hex is a focused magical act intended to cause disruption, discomfort, or retribution to a target. These spells often draw on darker energies, requiring immense control and responsibility. Key aspects of curses and hexes include:

1. **Retributive Energy**: These spells should be used only when justified, such as in cases of harm or injustice.
2. **Clear Intent**: Ambiguous intentions can lead to unintended consequences, so clarity is essential.
3. **Ethical Reflection**: Consider the moral and karmic implications before casting. Reflect on whether your goal aligns with your highest values.

Advanced Spells for Retribution and Hexing

These spells are designed to deliver consequences for harm or injustice. Use them only as a last resort and with caution.

1. The Mirror Curse

The mirror curse reflects a person's harmful actions or intentions back onto them, ensuring they face the consequences of their deeds.

Ingredients:

- A small mirror
- A black candle
- A piece of black cloth

Steps:

1. Light the black candle and place the mirror in front of it.
2. Focus on the harm or injustice caused by the target and visualize it returning to them, not as vengeance but as a reflection of their actions.
3. Say: *"Mirror bright, your deeds I show,*
   Back to you, let justice flow.
   What you send, you now shall see,
   The harm you caused returns to thee."
4. Wrap the mirror in the black cloth and store it in a safe place. Destroy the mirror after the curse is lifted.

2. The Thorn Hex

This hex creates discomfort and blocks negative actions without causing severe harm.

Ingredients:

- A thorny branch or dried thorns
- A black candle
- A piece of paper and pen

Steps:

1. Write the target's name and their harmful actions on the paper.
2. Wrap the paper in the thorny branch, binding it tightly as you visualize their harmful energy being restrained.
3. Light the black candle and say: *"Thorns of justice, sharp and keen,*
   Your harm is bound, your actions seen.
   Let this hex be firm and true,
   Until your harm no more breaks through."
4. Bury the thorn bundle away from your home to anchor the spell.

3. The Ashes of Silence Curse

This curse silences those who spread lies, gossip, or harm through words.

Ingredients:

- A piece of paper
- A black or gray candle
- A fireproof dish

Steps:

1. Write the name of the person and their harmful words on the paper.
2. Light the candle and burn the paper in the fireproof dish, saying:
   "Words of harm, lies and spite,
   Burn to ash, removed from sight.
   By this flame, your voice shall cease,
   Until you speak with truth and peace."
3. Scatter the ashes at a crossroads to seal the curse.

Methods of Breaking Curses or Reversing Hexes

Breaking curses or reversing hexes is essential when dealing with malevolent energy directed toward you. These spells neutralize or return the negative energy to its source.

1. Egg Cleansing Ritual

Egg cleansing removes curses and hexes by absorbing negative energy.

Ingredients:

- A raw egg
- A glass of water
- A white candle

Steps:

1. Light the white candle to create a sacred space.
2. Hold the egg in your hands and roll it over your body, focusing on absorbing all negative energy.
3. Crack the egg into the glass of water. Examine the patterns in the water; unusual shapes or bubbles may indicate a curse.
4. Dispose of the egg and water far from your home, saying:
   "Cleansed and pure, the curse is gone,
   By this act, I move on.
   Harm removed, my light restored,
   Protected now, forevermore."

2. Reversal Spell with a Black Candle

This spell sends a curse or hex back to its source.

Ingredients:

- A black candle
- A small mirror
- A pinch of salt

Steps:

1. Place the black candle in front of the mirror and sprinkle salt around both as a protective barrier.
2. Light the candle and visualize the negative energy returning to its sender, accompanied by a lesson to change their ways.
3. Say: *"By this mirror, I reflect,*
   Harmful energy, redirect.
   Back to sender, lessons learned,
   Balance restored, tables turned."
4. Let the candle burn down safely, then cleanse the space with sage or palo santo.

3. Protective Bath to Break a Curse

This bath ritual cleanses your energy and removes lingering hexes.

Ingredients:

- Sea salt
- Dried rosemary and basil
- A few drops of lavender or eucalyptus essential oil

Steps:

1. Draw a warm bath and add the salt, herbs, and essential oil.
2. Sit in the bath and visualize the water washing away all negative energy.
3. Say: *"By water's flow, by herb and stone,*
   This curse is broken, I stand alone.
   Cleansed and free, my spirit whole,
   Protection surrounds my heart and soul."
4. Drain the bath, imagining all negativity disappearing with the water.

Warnings About the Consequences of Dark Magic

Dark magic, including curses and hexes, carries significant risks. Consider the following warnings before engaging in this work:

1. The Rule of Three

Many traditions, including Wicca, believe that energy you send out returns to you threefold. Misusing curses or hexes can result in karmic repercussions.

2. Emotional Drain

Casting dark magic can drain your energy and lead to spiritual imbalance. Always cleanse yourself and your space after performing such spells.

3. Ethical Accountability

Even justified curses can have unintended consequences. Reflect on whether the spell aligns with your values and whether there are non-magical solutions to the problem.

4. Protection First

Before working with dark magic, ensure you have strong protective measures in place to guard against spiritual retaliation.

Conclusion

Curses and hexes are powerful tools in magic, capable of addressing harm and injustice when used responsibly. However, they demand careful consideration, respect for ethical boundaries, and awareness of their potential consequences. Balancing these practices with methods to break curses and protect against harm ensures a measured and thoughtful approach to dark magic. Let your work be guided by wisdom, clarity, and respect for the balance of energy in the universe.

Chapter 19: Healing with Voodoo Magic

Voodoo healing magic draws upon the energies of nature, the spiritual realm, and personal intent to address physical, emotional, and spiritual ailments. Rooted in a deep respect for the interconnectedness of all things, Voodoo healing rituals and spells incorporate herbs, oils, charms, and the guidance of the Loa to restore balance and promote well-being. In this chapter, we explore powerful healing practices, spells for protection from illness, and charms for enhancing mental clarity and spiritual health.

The Philosophy of Voodoo Healing Magic

Healing in Voodoo is holistic, addressing the physical, emotional, and spiritual dimensions of well-being. Core principles include:

1. **Nature's Wisdom**: Herbs, roots, and oils carry potent energies that align with specific healing purposes.
2. **Spiritual Guidance**: The Loa and ancestral spirits are called upon to support healing and offer guidance.
3. **Balance and Harmony**: Illness is often viewed as a disruption of energy, and healing seeks to restore equilibrium.

Rituals Using Herbs, Oils, and Spiritual Energy for Healing

These rituals harness the power of natural and spiritual elements to heal physical and emotional wounds.

1. Herbal Healing Ritual for Physical Ailments

This ritual uses the healing properties of herbs and spiritual energy to support recovery from illness.

Ingredients:

- A white candle
- Dried chamomile, rosemary, and thyme
- A bowl of warm water
- A small towel

Steps:

1. Light the white candle to symbolize purity and healing energy.
2. Add the dried herbs to the bowl of warm water, allowing their essence to infuse.
3. Dip the towel into the herbal water and gently place it on the affected area (if applicable) or over your forehead.
4. Say: *"Herbs of Earth, bring your cure,*
   Healing power, strong and pure.
   Restore my body, make me whole,
   Heal my spirit, mind, and soul."
5. Repeat the ritual daily until relief is achieved.

2. Spiritual Cleansing with Florida Water

Florida Water, a traditional Voodoo cleansing tool, is used to purify the aura and release emotional burdens.

Ingredients:

- Florida Water or a homemade blend (alcohol, orange peel, lavender, and clove)
- A bowl of water
- A white cloth

Steps:

1. Add a few drops of Florida Water to the bowl of water.
2. Dip the white cloth into the mixture and gently wipe your face, hands, and chest while saying: *"Spirit pure, cleanse my pain,*
   Wash away all harm and strain.
   Renew my energy, fresh and bright,
   Fill my soul with healing light."
3. Allow the water to dry naturally on your skin to seal the cleansing.

3. Emotional Healing with Rose and Lavender

This ritual focuses on soothing emotional wounds and fostering self-love.

Ingredients:

- A pink or white candle
- A bowl of dried rose petals and lavender
- A rose quartz crystal

Steps:

1. Light the candle and sit comfortably with the bowl of herbs and rose quartz in front of you.
2. Hold the rose quartz to your heart and say: *"Rose and lavender, calm and kind,*
   Heal my heart, soothe my mind.
   Let love flow, let pain release,
   Bring me comfort, bring me peace."
3. Meditate for 10–15 minutes, focusing on releasing emotional pain and welcoming self-love.

Spells for Protection from Illness and Disease

Preventive magic creates an energetic barrier against illness, shielding you from harm while strengthening your natural defenses.

1. Protection Oil Spell

This spell creates a protective oil to anoint yourself or your space against illness.

Ingredients:

- Olive oil or coconut oil
- Dried basil, eucalyptus, and rosemary
- A small glass bottle

Steps:

1. Combine the oil and herbs in the bottle, focusing on your intention for protection.
2. Hold the bottle and say: *"Oil of health, ward off disease,*
   Protect my body, bring me ease.
   By this blend, I stay secure,
   Safe and strong, my health is sure."
3. Anoint your wrists, neck, or home entryways with the oil.

2. Healing Ward Spell

This spell creates a ward around your home to protect against illness.

Ingredients:

- A black tourmaline or obsidian stone
- A bowl of salt
- A green or white candle

Steps:

1. Place the stone in the bowl of salt and light the candle nearby.
2. Say: *"Ward of health, strong and clear,*
   Protect this home from what draws near.
   Illness flees, no harm shall stay,
   This sacred space is safe today."
3. Keep the bowl near your front door or a central location in your home.

Charms for Enhancing Mental Clarity and Spiritual Well-Being

These charms focus on maintaining balance and fostering mental and spiritual clarity.

1. Mental Clarity Charm

This charm sharpens focus and clears mental fog, ideal for times of stress or confusion.

Ingredients:

- A small pouch
- Dried peppermint and bay leaves
- A clear quartz crystal

Steps:

1. Fill the pouch with the herbs and crystal, focusing on your intention for clarity and focus.
2. Hold the pouch and say: *"Mind of sharpness, clear and bright,*
   Focus strong, my guiding light.
   By this charm, my thoughts align,
   My clarity and strength are mine."
3. Carry the charm with you or place it on your desk while working.

2. Spiritual Balance Talisman

This talisman fosters inner peace and spiritual harmony.

Ingredients:

- A silver or blue pendant
- A piece of selenite
- A strand of white thread

Steps:

1. Wrap the selenite with the thread and attach it to the pendant.
2. Hold the talisman and say: *"Balance flows, as spirits blend,*
   My inner peace shall never end.
   Guided by light, my soul is free,
   Harmony dwells inside of me."
3. Wear the talisman during meditation or stressful situations.

Maintaining Your Healing Magic

- **Consistency**: Healing magic works best when practiced regularly. Incorporate rituals and charms into your daily routine.
- **Gratitude**: Thank the herbs, oils, and spirits you work with for their assistance, offering small tokens of appreciation like flowers or incense.
- **Self-Care**: Combine magic with practical self-care, such as eating healthily, resting, and seeking medical advice when necessary.

Conclusion

Healing with Voodoo magic is a powerful way to restore balance, protect against harm, and nurture emotional and spiritual well-being. By using herbs, oils, and spiritual energy, you create a holistic approach to health that honors both the physical and metaphysical aspects of healing. Let your intentions guide your practice, and trust in the wisdom of nature and spirit to bring renewal and strength.

Chapter 20: The Spells of Shadow and Light

Magic, like nature and life, operates in a balance of dualities—light and shadow, creation and destruction, harmony and chaos. The magic of shadow and light teaches us that embracing this duality is essential to mastering our craft and understanding our inner selves. This chapter explores spells and rituals that harmonize white and black magic, offer tools for mastering control of opposing forces, and provide charms for navigating inner darkness to uncover the light.

The Dual Nature of Magic

Magic is neither inherently good nor evil; it reflects the intention and energy of the practitioner. The duality of shadow and light serves as a metaphor for the choices we make and the energies we align with. Key principles include:

1. **Balance**: Effective magic requires an understanding of both shadow (confronting challenges, setting boundaries) and light (nurturing, creating harmony).
2. **Responsibility**: Mastery comes with the ethical use of both energies, ensuring your actions align with your values.
3. **Integration**: Shadow and light exist within every individual. Embracing both allows for wholeness and deeper understanding.

Balancing Spells Using Both White and Black Magic

These spells harmonize opposing forces, helping practitioners wield both energies responsibly and effectively.

1. Shadow and Light Harmony Spell

This spell aligns the energies of shadow and light within yourself and your magical practice.

Ingredients:

- A white candle and a black candle
- A clear quartz crystal
- A piece of parchment and pen

Steps:

1. Place the white and black candles side by side, with the quartz crystal between them.
2. Light both candles and say: *"Shadow and light, balanced and whole,*
   Together as one, I reach my goal.
   Darkness protects, light will create,
   Both I honor, both I embrace."
3. Write your intention on the parchment, clearly stating how you wish to harmonize these energies.
4. Fold the parchment and place it under the quartz crystal. Let the candles burn down safely.
5. Keep the crystal as a talisman of balance.

2. Lunar Equilibrium Spell

This spell uses the phases of the Moon to balance shadow and light energies.

Ingredients:

- A silver candle (symbolizing light) and a dark gray candle (symbolizing shadow)
- A bowl of water
- A silver coin

Steps:

1. Place the candles on either side of the bowl of water and the silver coin in the center of the bowl.
2. Light both candles and say: *"By waxing moon and waning phase, I call balance to light my ways. Shadow deep, and silver glow, Harmonize my path; together flow."*
3. Focus on the reflection of the candles in the water, visualizing your energies balancing.
4. Keep the coin as a charm for maintaining equilibrium in your life.

Rituals for Embracing the Dual Nature of Magic and Mastering Control

To master the interplay of shadow and light, you must understand their strengths and limitations, learning to wield both with discipline and wisdom.

1. Shadow Integration Ritual

This ritual helps you confront and embrace your inner shadows, turning fear or negativity into strength.

Ingredients:

- A black mirror or dark bowl filled with water
- A black candle
- A piece of obsidian or smoky quartz

Steps:

1. Light the black candle and place the mirror or bowl in front of you.
2. Hold the obsidian and gaze into the reflective surface, focusing on your inner fears, doubts, or suppressed emotions.
3. Say: *"Shadow within, I do not fear,*
   Your lessons deep, I hold you near.
   Strength from darkness, wisdom true,
   I accept and transform through you."
4. Allow yourself to process any emotions that arise. When ready, extinguish the candle and cleanse yourself with a sage or palo santo smudging.

2. Light Mastery Ritual

This ritual focuses on amplifying your ability to channel and create positive energy.

Ingredients:

- A white or gold candle
- A bowl of clear water
- A small piece of sunstone

Steps:

1. Light the white or gold candle and place the bowl of water in front of it.
2. Hold the sunstone and focus on its warmth, visualizing light energy filling your entire being.
3. Say: *"Light within, radiant and pure,*
   Strength to create, to heal, and endure.
   I channel your power, bright and true,
   A beacon of light in all I do."
4. Dip your fingers into the water and anoint your forehead, heart, and palms as symbols of your connection to light.

Charms for Dealing with Inner Darkness and Finding the Light

These charms help navigate periods of emotional or spiritual struggle, offering guidance and illumination.

1. Shadow Guardian Charm

This charm protects and empowers you during times of emotional darkness or spiritual challenge.

Ingredients:

- A small pouch
- Dried rosemary and thyme
- A piece of onyx or jet stone

Steps:

1. Place the herbs and stone into the pouch, focusing on their protective and grounding qualities.
2. Hold the pouch and say: *"Guardian of shadow, strong and wise,*
   Protect my soul, where darkness lies.
   Guide me safely through the night,
   To find my way back to the light."
3. Carry the charm with you during difficult times.

2. Light-Seeker's Talisman

This talisman helps you maintain hope and clarity during challenging moments.

Ingredients:

- A small silver charm or key
- A strand of white thread
- A piece of clear quartz

Steps:

1. Wrap the silver charm or key with the white thread, tying the quartz to it.
2. Hold the talisman and say: *"Key of light, guide my way,*
   Through darkest night and troubled day.
   My path is clear, my hope is strong,
   The light returns, where I belong."
3. Wear or carry the talisman to stay connected to hope and clarity.

Ethical Considerations in Balancing Shadow and Light

Mastery of shadow and light magic requires careful reflection and accountability. Keep the following in mind:

1. **Self-Awareness**: Regularly examine your intentions to ensure your work aligns with your highest self.
2. **Respect for Others**: Balance does not mean justifying harm; use shadow energy responsibly and only when necessary.
3. **Harmony Over Extremes**: Avoid over-reliance on either shadow or light. Both serve a purpose and should work in tandem.

Conclusion

The magic of shadow and light offers profound insights into the nature of balance, control, and transformation. By mastering these dual forces, you gain the ability to navigate life's complexities with wisdom and strength. Embrace the lessons of darkness and the guidance of light, allowing both to coexist in harmony within your magical practice and daily life. Through balance, you find the path to true mastery.

Chapter 21: Ultimate Power: The Forbidden Spells

The ultimate power within magic lies in its ability to invoke forces beyond the mundane, channeling energies that shape reality itself. Forbidden spells, as their name implies, are not for the faint of heart or casual practitioners. They tap into potent, often volatile energies that require utmost caution, preparation, and respect. In this chapter, we delve into advanced spells for summoning great power, rituals invoking the spirits of Rose Hall, and curses and charms reserved for the most dire circumstances. This is a realm of magic that demands responsibility, reverence, and unshakable resolve.

The Nature of Forbidden Magic

Forbidden magic exists at the boundaries of what is considered safe or ethical. These spells often deal with forces that can be unpredictable or overwhelming if improperly handled. Key principles include:

1. **Caution and Control**: Mastery over your own energy and intent is vital to avoid unintended consequences.
2. **Respect for Spirits**: When working with powerful entities, including the spirits of Rose Hall, reverence and offerings are non-negotiable.
3. **Preparation and Grounding**: Before engaging in forbidden spells, ensure you are physically, emotionally, and spiritually grounded.

Spells for Summoning Great Power

These spells draw on immense energies to achieve extraordinary outcomes. They are meant for experienced practitioners who understand the risks involved.

1. The Spell of Invincible Will

This spell amplifies your inner strength and determination, allowing you to overcome obstacles with unshakable resolve.

Ingredients:

- A gold candle and a black candle
- A piece of obsidian
- A drop of your own blood (or a symbolic alternative, like red wine)

Steps:

1. Place the gold and black candles on either side of the obsidian, symbolizing the balance of creation and destruction.
2. Light both candles and focus on the obsidian, visualizing it absorbing your intention for invincible willpower.
3. Prick your finger to release a single drop of blood onto the stone (or use the alternative), saying: *"By shadow deep and golden fire,*
   My will is forged, my strength entire.
   No force can break, no storm shall sway,
   My power grows, night and day."
4. Carry the obsidian as a talisman of your strengthened will.

2. The Elemental Summoning Spell

This spell calls upon the raw forces of Earth, Air, Fire, and Water to infuse your magic with their power.

Ingredients:

- A bowl of earth, a feather, a candle, and a bowl of water
- A silver ring or other personal item
- A black or red cord

Steps:

1. Arrange the items to represent the four elements, placing your personal item in the center.
2. Tie the cord around the personal item, knotting it tightly as you say: *"Earth, my foundation; Air, my breath,*
   Fire, my passion; Water, my depth.
   Spirits of elements, hear my plea,
   Lend your power, flow through me."
3. Carry or wear the empowered item when performing high-level spells.

Rituals Invoking the Spirits of Rose Hall

The spirits tied to Rose Hall hold immense energy and knowledge, offering guidance, protection, or even strength. Approach them with respect, as their temperaments can range from benevolent to vengeful.

1. The Ritual of Annie Palmer's Wisdom

Invoke the legendary White Witch of Rose Hall for insight, power, and strength in decision-making.

Ingredients:

- A black candle and a white candle
- A piece of silver jewelry (offering to Annie Palmer)
- A mirror

Steps:

1. Light the black and white candles, placing the mirror between them to act as a portal.
2. Hold the silver jewelry in your hands and say: *"Annie Palmer, witch of might,*
   I seek your wisdom this sacred night.
   Share your strength, your secrets deep,
   Guide my path while shadows sleep."
3. Place the jewelry in front of the mirror as an offering and gaze into the mirror, observing any impressions or images that appear.
4. When finished, bury the jewelry near a tree or crossroads to complete the offering.

2. The Spirit Guardian Ritual

Summon a protective spirit from Rose Hall to guard you or your space.

Ingredients:

- A bowl of salt
- A silver or black candle
- A token from Rose Hall (or a symbolic substitute, such as a black feather)

Steps:

1. Create a circle of salt around yourself or the space you wish to protect.
2. Light the candle and hold the token, focusing on your request for protection.
3. Say: *"Spirit strong of Rose Hall's land,*
   Guard this space by your command.
   Let no harm or ill draw near,
   Protect this place; my call you hear."
4. Leave the token at the edge of your property or in the center of your protected space.

Curses and Charms Meant Only for Dire Circumstances

These powerful tools are reserved for situations of extreme necessity, where harm or injustice must be addressed.

1. The Curse of Absolute Justice

This curse ensures that those who harm others are brought to justice by the forces they cannot escape.

Ingredients:

- A photograph or representation of the target
- A black candle
- A piece of broken glass

Steps:

1. Light the black candle and place the photograph or representation in front of it.
2. Hold the broken glass and say: *"Justice calls, no escape,*
   By your deeds, your fate I shape.
   Harm repaid, by power and might,
   Justice served, in shadow and light."
3. Place the broken glass over the photograph and bury them together in the ground, sealing the curse.

2. The Charm of Lasting Protection

This charm safeguards against retaliation or harm from malevolent forces.

Ingredients:

- A small pouch
- A piece of obsidian or onyx
- Dried basil and salt

Steps:

1. Fill the pouch with the obsidian, basil, and salt, focusing on creating an impenetrable shield.
2. Hold the pouch and say: *"By this charm, my path is clear,*
   No harm shall touch, no ill draw near.
   Shield me now, both day and night,
   Protected strong, by shadow and light."
3. Keep the pouch on your person during times of potential danger.

Warnings About Forbidden Spells

1. **Karmic Consequences**: The more powerful the spell, the greater the risk of unintended backlash. Consider the ethical implications of your actions.
2. **Spiritual Fatigue**: Forbidden magic can drain your energy and leave you vulnerable. Always cleanse and ground yourself afterward.
3. **Respect Boundaries**: Never use these spells frivolously or without clear justification. They are tools of last resort, not casual practices.

Conclusion

The forbidden spells of shadow and light offer access to immense power, but they demand great responsibility, respect, and mastery. By summoning spirits, harmonizing dual energies, or invoking powerful curses and charms, you tap into forces capable of transforming your life and circumstances. Approach these practices with caution, clarity, and reverence, and they will serve as a testament to your growth and discipline in the magical arts. Use these spells wisely, for ultimate power comes with ultimate accountability.

Appendix A: Glossary

This glossary provides detailed definitions of the magical terms, ingredients, and concepts referenced throughout *The White Witch of Rose Hall's Spellbook*. It serves as a comprehensive guide for readers to deepen their understanding of the practices, tools, and philosophies presented in the book.

A

- **Amulet**: A magical object worn or carried for protection or to bring good fortune. Amulets are often infused with specific intentions and energies.
- **Astral Travel**: The practice of projecting one's consciousness beyond the physical body to explore spiritual or astral realms.
- **Anointing**: The act of applying oil or another substance to an object or person to consecrate or empower them with magical energy.

B

- **Banishing**: A ritual or spell designed to remove negative energies, entities, or influences from a space, object, or individual.
- **Binding**: A spell used to restrict or neutralize the harmful actions or influence of a person or spirit.
- **Black Magic**: A type of magic often associated with shadow work, curses, and spells that deal with darker energies. It is not inherently evil but must be used responsibly.

C

- **Candles**: Common tools in magic that represent fire and are used to focus energy and intention. Candle colors have specific correspondences (e.g., white for purity, black for protection).

- **Circle Casting**: The act of creating a sacred, protected space for magical or spiritual work.
- **Clairvoyance**: The ability to perceive information or events beyond normal sensory input, often through visions or intuitive impressions.
- **Cleansing**: The process of removing negative or stagnant energy from a person, object, or space, often using tools like sage, salt, or water.
- **Curse**: A spell intended to bring harm or misfortune to a person or place. Curses are powerful and carry significant ethical considerations.

D

- **Divination**: The practice of seeking insight or guidance from spiritual or mystical means, such as tarot cards, runes, or scrying mirrors.
- **Dream Magic**: The use of spells, charms, or rituals to influence or harness the power of dreams for guidance, prophecy, or spiritual connection.
- **Duality**: The concept of balance between opposing forces, such as light and shadow, creation and destruction, or good and evil.

E

- **Elements**: The foundational forces of nature in magic—Earth, Air, Fire, and Water—each representing different energies and correspondences.
- **Energy Work**: The practice of manipulating or channeling energy to achieve a desired outcome in magical or spiritual practices.
- **Equilibrium**: The state of balance between energies or forces, often sought in spells and rituals.

F

- **Familiar**: A spiritual entity, often appearing as an animal, that assists a witch in their magical practice.
- **Florida Water**: A cologne used in Voodoo and other magical traditions for cleansing, protection, and spiritual work.
- **Full Moon**: The lunar phase when the Moon is fully illuminated. It is a time of heightened energy, often used for spells of manifestation, completion, and abundance.

G

- **Gris-Gris Bag**: A small charm bag used in Voodoo to carry herbs, stones, or other magical items for protection, luck, or specific intentions.
- **Grounding**: The practice of connecting to the Earth's energy to stabilize and balance one's own energy.

H

- **Herbs**: Plants used in magic for their energetic properties. Examples include lavender for peace, basil for prosperity, and rosemary for protection.
- **Hex**: A spell intended to cause discomfort or obstacles for a target. Like curses, hexes should be used with caution and ethical reflection.

I

- **Incantation**: A verbal expression of magical intent, often in the form of a chant or rhyme.
- **Intent**: The focus and purpose behind a spell or ritual, which directs the energy toward a specific goal.

J

- **Justice Spells**: Spells aimed at bringing balance or fairness, often used to address harm or wrongdoing.

L

- **Light Magic**: A type of magic that focuses on healing, protection, and positive transformation.
- **Loa**: Powerful spirits in Voodoo who act as intermediaries between humans and the divine. Examples include Erzulie Freda (love) and Damballa (fertility).

M

- **Manifestation**: The act of bringing a desired outcome into reality through focused energy, intention, and action.
- **Moon Phases**: The cyclical changes of the Moon, each phase carrying unique energies for magical work (e.g., New Moon for new beginnings, Waning Moon for banishing).

N

- **Necromancy**: The practice of communicating with the dead for guidance, insight, or spiritual assistance.
- **New Moon**: The lunar phase when the Moon is not visible, symbolizing new beginnings and fresh starts in magic.

O

- **Obsidian**: A black volcanic glass used for protection, grounding, and scrying.

- **Offering**: A gift presented to spirits, deities, or ancestors during rituals to show respect and request their aid.

P

- **Pendulum**: A divination tool, often a weighted object on a string or chain, used to receive yes/no answers or guidance.
- **Protection Spell**: A spell designed to create a shield of energy around a person, object, or space to ward off harm.

R

- **Rose Hall**: A historical plantation in Jamaica associated with the legend of Annie Palmer, the White Witch of Rose Hall, who is said to possess immense magical power.
- **Runes**: Ancient symbols used for divination, each carrying unique meanings and energies.

S

- **Salt**: A purifying and protective substance often used in magical practices to cleanse or create protective barriers.
- **Scrying**: The practice of gazing into a reflective surface, such as a mirror or water, to receive visions or insights.
- **Servitor**: A thought-form or spirit created by a practitioner for a specific purpose, such as protection or guidance.
- **Sigil**: A symbol imbued with magical intent, often created by condensing a written intention into a unique design.

T

- **Talismans**: Objects charged with specific energy to attract or amplify a desired outcome, such as luck, health, or love.

- **Tarot Cards**: A divination tool consisting of 78 cards, each carrying symbolic meanings that provide guidance and insight.

V

- **Veve**: Sacred symbols used in Voodoo rituals to invoke specific Loa.
- **Voodoo**: A spiritual tradition originating in West Africa and the Caribbean, blending ancestral, natural, and divine energies for magical practices.

W

- **Warding**: The act of creating an energetic shield to protect against negative influences or entities.
- **Waxing Moon**: The lunar phase between the New Moon and Full Moon, associated with growth and manifestation.
- **Waning Moon**: The lunar phase between the Full Moon and New Moon, associated with banishing and release.

Y

- **Yarrow**: A healing herb used for protection, courage, and psychic development.

Z

- **Zombi**: In Voodoo lore, a reanimated being or spirit. The term symbolizes the intersection of life, death, and magic.

This glossary serves as a foundational resource for practitioners, providing clarity and deeper understanding of the magical terms and concepts used throughout the book. Use it to enhance your practice and navigate the rich, complex world of the White Witch of Rose Hall's magic.

Appendix B: Herbal Index

This herbal index provides a comprehensive list of herbs and plants referenced throughout *The White Witch of Rose Hall's Spellbook*. Each entry includes the magical properties, traditional uses, and guidance for incorporating these potent botanicals into your spells and rituals.

A

- **Alfalfa**

  Properties: Prosperity, protection from poverty, anti-hunger spells.

  Uses: Place in a small jar in your pantry to ward off financial difficulties. Use in prosperity charms and rituals for abundance.

- **Aloe Vera**

  Properties: Healing, protection, emotional balance.

  Uses: Keep a live aloe plant in your home to protect against negativity. Use the sap in healing ointments or bath rituals.

- **Angelica Root**

  Properties: Protection, purification, divine connection.

  Uses: Burn as incense to purify a space. Carry as a talisman to guard against malevolent spirits.

B

- **Basil**

  Properties: Prosperity, love, protection.

  Uses: Add to charm bags or sprinkle around your home for wealth and harmony. Use in love potions or reconciliation spells.

- **Bay Leaves**

  Properties: Protection, wishes, success.

Uses: Write your wishes on a bay leaf and burn it to release the intention. Add to baths for spiritual cleansing.

- **Black Cohosh**
  Properties: Strength, courage, protection.
  Uses: Use in rituals to boost personal power or as an ingredient in protective spells.

C

- **Calendula (Marigold)**
  Properties: Happiness, protection, prophetic dreams.
  Uses: Scatter petals around your home for joy and safety. Use in dream sachets to enhance intuition.
- **Camomile**
  Properties: Peace, sleep, luck, purification.
  Uses: Brew into tea to calm the mind and attract good luck. Add to dream pillows for restful sleep.
- **Cinnamon**
  Properties: Prosperity, passion, energy.
  Uses: Sprinkle powdered cinnamon in your wallet for financial gain. Burn as incense to amplify energy during rituals.
- **Clove**
  Properties: Protection, courage, banishing.
  Uses: Burn to banish negativity or wear in a charm to boost confidence.

D

- **Dandelion**
  Properties: Divination, wishes, cleansing.
  Uses: Use the seeds in wish spells. Brew into tea to enhance psychic abilities.

- **Devil's Claw**
  Properties: Protection, reversing curses, strength.
  Uses: Carry as a talisman to ward off harm. Use in spells to break curses or hexes.

E

- **Eucalyptus**
  Properties: Healing, purification, protection.
  Uses: Burn the leaves to cleanse a space. Use in baths to recover from illness or emotional strain.

F

- **Fennel**
  Properties: Courage, longevity, protection.
  Uses: Hang over doorways to repel negative energy. Brew into tea for personal empowerment.
- **Frankincense**
  Properties: Purification, spiritual connection, protection.
  Uses: Burn as incense to raise vibrations and cleanse spaces.

G

- **Garlic**
  Properties: Protection, warding off evil, purification.
  Uses: Hang in your home to repel malevolent forces. Use in banishing rituals for spiritual cleansing.
- **Ginger**
  Properties: Power, energy, love.
  Uses: Add to spells to amplify their power. Use in attraction spells to spark passion.

H

- **Hibiscus**
  Properties: Love, passion, attraction.
  Uses: Use in love spells or potions. Add to baths to enhance allure and confidence.
- **Honeysuckle**
  Properties: Prosperity, psychic powers.
  Uses: Place in your wallet for financial gain. Burn to enhance psychic abilities during divination.

J

- **Jasmine**
  Properties: Love, prophetic dreams, serenity.
  Uses: Add to dream pillows for enhanced intuition. Use in love potions or spells for spiritual connection.
- **Juniper Berries**
  Properties: Protection, purification, health.
  Uses: Burn to cleanse a space or ward off illness. Carry in a pouch for personal safety.

L

- **Lavender**
  Properties: Peace, love, protection, sleep.
  Uses: Burn as incense to promote relaxation. Use in sachets or baths for restful sleep and emotional balance.
- **Lemon Balm**
  Properties: Healing, love, success.
  Uses: Brew into tea for emotional clarity and stress relief. Add to spells for success and happiness.

M

- **Mugwort**
  Properties: Psychic power, astral travel, protection.
  Uses: Burn as incense to enhance divination. Place under your pillow to encourage lucid dreaming and astral projection.
- **Mint**
  Properties: Prosperity, protection, clarity.
  Uses: Add to charm bags for financial success. Brew into tea to clear the mind and focus energy.

R

- **Rosemary**
  Properties: Protection, memory, purification.
  Uses: Burn to cleanse a space or enhance memory. Use in spells to protect your home and loved ones.
- **Rue**
  Properties: Cleansing, protection, breaking curses.
  Uses: Add to baths to cleanse spiritual residue. Use in rituals to break hexes or curses.

S

- **Sage**
  Properties: Purification, wisdom, protection.
  Uses: Burn to cleanse spaces and objects. Use in rituals to seek wisdom and clarity.
- **St. John's Wort**
  Properties: Protection, strength, happiness.
  Uses: Carry to ward off negative spirits. Use in spells to boost courage and positivity.

T

- **Thyme**
  Properties: Courage, health, purification.
  Uses: Burn to purify a space or boost courage. Use in healing spells for resilience and recovery.

V

- **Valerian Root**
  Properties: Sleep, peace, protection.
  Uses: Add to sachets or baths for restful sleep. Use in rituals to calm tension or promote harmony.
- **Vervain**
  Properties: Protection, purification, creativity.
  Uses: Use in rituals to cleanse energy. Carry to inspire creativity and focus.

Y

- **Yarrow**
  Properties: Courage, protection, love.
  Uses: Add to charm bags for courage. Use in rituals to strengthen emotional bonds or protect relationships.

Conclusion

This herbal index highlights the versatility and potency of plants in magical practice. By understanding the unique properties of each herb, you can tailor your spells and rituals to align with your specific intentions. Always approach herbal magic with respect, gratitude, and care, ensuring a deep connection with the natural world.

Appendix C: Astrological Charts

This appendix provides comprehensive tables for lunar phases, planetary movements, and celestial events, offering a detailed reference to enhance your magical practices. Understanding and aligning your spells and rituals with celestial energies allows you to harness the natural rhythms of the universe for greater potency and precision.

Lunar Phases: 2024 Calendar

The Moon's phases influence magical work, with each phase carrying unique energies suited for specific intentions. Below is a table outlining the key lunar phases for 2024:

Date	Phase	Magical Focus
Jan 11	New Moon	New beginnings, intention setting, manifesting.
Jan 25	Full Moon	Abundance, completion, illumination.
Feb 9	New Moon	Planting seeds, starting new projects.
Feb 24	Full Moon	Emotional clarity, achieving goals.
Mar 10	New Moon	Inner reflection, planning future actions.
Mar 24	Full Moon	Celebrations, peak energy for spellcasting.
Apr 8	New Moon	Quiet contemplation, healing past wounds.

Date	Phase	Magical Focus
Apr 23	Full Moon	Harvesting rewards, spiritual growth.
May 8	New Moon	Manifesting financial abundance, creating opportunities.
May 23	Full Moon	Empowerment, gratitude for success.

Planetary Movements: Retrogrades and Alignments in 2024

Planetary retrogrades and alignments are pivotal in astrology, influencing energies on Earth. The following chart highlights major planetary events for 2024:

Planet	Retrograde Period	Impact
Mercury	Apr 1 – Apr 25	Communication issues, delays in travel.
Venus	Jul 22 – Sept 3	Challenges in love, reassessment of values.
Mars	Oct 10 – Dec 14	Reduced energy, introspection on ambitions.
Jupiter	Jun 10 – Oct 22	Reevaluation of growth, slowing expansion.
Saturn	Feb 14 – Jun 26	Discipline, restructuring long-term plans.
Uranus	Aug 1 – Dec 16	Unexpected change, innovation blocks.

Celestial Events: 2024 Highlights

Celestial events such as eclipses, meteor showers, and planetary alignments bring heightened spiritual energy, making them ideal for specific magical workings. Below is a chart of key celestial events:

Date	Event	Magical Focus
Mar 20	Spring Equinox	Balance, new beginnings, fertility magic.
Apr 8	Total Solar Eclipse	Transformation, breaking patterns, new cycles.
Jun 21	Summer Solstice	Celebration, abundance, energy for passion spells.
Aug 12–13	Perseid Meteor Shower	Wish spells, connecting with cosmic energies.
Sept 23	Autumn Equinox	Harvest, gratitude, preparing for introspection.
Oct 17	Partial Lunar Eclipse	Releasing emotional baggage, deep introspection.
Dec 21	Winter Solstice	Protection, reflection, setting intentions for the new year.

Planetary Days and Their Correspondences

Each day of the week is ruled by a planet, which influences the type of magic that is most effective. Use this chart to align your rituals with the planetary energies:

Day	Ruling Planet	Magical Focus
Monday	Moon	Intuition, emotions, dreams, healing.
Tuesday	Mars	Courage, strength, conflict resolution.
Wednesday	Mercury	Communication, travel, intellectual pursuits.
Thursday	Jupiter	Abundance, prosperity, expansion.
Friday	Venus	Love, beauty, harmony, relationships.
Saturday	Saturn	Discipline, protection, banishing negativity.
Sunday	Sun	Success, vitality, creativity, personal power.

Astrological Moon Sign Calendar

The Moon's transit through zodiac signs impacts the emotional and energetic tone of each day. This table outlines the best magical focuses for each Moon sign:

Moon Sign	Magical Focus
Aries	Courage, ambition, initiating new projects.
Taurus	Stability, abundance, financial matters.
Gemini	Communication, adaptability, learning.
Cancer	Home, family, nurturing, emotional healing.
Leo	Creativity, self-expression, leadership.
Virgo	Organization, health, practical concerns.
Libra	Relationships, balance, beauty, legal matters.
Scorpio	Transformation, deep emotions, protection.
Sagittarius	Adventure, higher learning, spiritual growth.
Capricorn	Career, long-term planning, discipline.

Moon Sign	Magical Focus
Aquarius	Innovation, community, independence.
Pisces	Intuition, dreams, psychic development, compassion.

Using the Charts

1. **Spell Timing**: Plan your rituals and spells around the lunar phases and planetary movements to align with the most supportive energies.
2. **Daily Work**: Incorporate the planetary day and Moon sign into your daily magical practice for ongoing alignment.
3. **Special Events**: Use celestial events for high-impact rituals, such as eclipses for transformation or solstices for powerful new beginnings.

This appendix serves as a vital resource for practitioners seeking to integrate astrological knowledge into their magical work. By synchronizing your practice with the celestial rhythms, you amplify the potency and precision of your intentions.

Appendix D: Further Reading

To deepen your understanding of Voodoo, witchcraft, and spellcraft traditions, this appendix provides a curated list of texts and resources. These books explore the history, philosophy, and practical applications of magic, offering invaluable insights for both beginners and advanced practitioners.

I. Voodoo and African Diaspora Traditions

1. ***Voodoo Queen: The Spirited Lives of Marie Laveau*** by Martha Ward
   - A comprehensive biography of Marie Laveau, the legendary Voodoo practitioner of New Orleans, this book explores her life, influence, and the broader cultural impact of Voodoo traditions.

2. ***Haitian Vodou: An Introduction to Haiti's Indigenous Spiritual Tradition*** by Mambo Chita Tann
   - This book provides an accessible overview of Haitian Vodou, including its rituals, spirits (Loa), and cultural significance.

3. ***The Haitian Vodou Handbook: Protocols for Riding with the Lwa*** by Kenaz Filan
   - A practical guide to working with the spirits in Vodou, this book includes advice on setting up altars, making offerings, and navigating the spiritual realm with respect and intention.

4. ***Mama Lola: A Vodou Priestess in Brooklyn*** by Karen McCarthy Brown

- ◦ This ethnographic account delves into the life of Mama Lola, a Vodou priestess, exploring her spiritual practices and the community she serves.

5. *Secrets of Voodoo* by Milo Rigaud
    - ◦ A detailed exploration of the origins, symbols, and ceremonies of Voodoo, offering a scholarly yet accessible introduction to the tradition.

II. Witchcraft and General Spellcraft

1. ***The Spiral Dance: A Rebirth of the Ancient Religion of the Great Goddess*** by Starhawk
   - A foundational text in modern witchcraft, this book explores the spiritual and political dimensions of Goddess worship, rituals, and magical practice.
2. ***The Complete Book of Witchcraft*** by Raymond Buckland
   - Often called "Buckland's Blue Book," this text offers a comprehensive guide to Wiccan practices, rituals, and tools for solitary or group practitioners.
3. ***Witchcraft: Theory and Practice*** by Ly de Angeles
   - A practical guide to spellcraft and magical workings, emphasizing the philosophical and energetic principles that underpin effective magic.
4. ***Cunningham's Encyclopedia of Magical Herbs*** by Scott Cunningham
   - A classic reference for herbal magic, this book includes detailed descriptions of magical properties, correspondences, and uses for hundreds of plants.
5. ***The Book of Spells: The Magick of Witchcraft*** by Jamie Della
   - A beginner-friendly book that explores the basics of spellcraft, including rituals, potions, and the ethical considerations of magical practice.

III. Advanced Magical Practices

1. *The Sorcerer's Secrets: Strategies in Practical Magick* by Jason Miller
   - A guide for advanced practitioners, this book explores practical magic with an emphasis on results-driven strategies and personal empowerment.
2. *High Magick: A Guide to the Spiritual Practices That Saved My Life on Death Row* by Damien Echols
   - This inspiring text combines autobiography with advanced teachings on ceremonial magic, meditation, and energy work.
3. *Modern Magick: Twelve Lessons in the High Magickal Arts* by Donald Michael Kraig
   - A comprehensive course in ceremonial magic, covering everything from basic techniques to advanced rituals and magical systems.

IV. Folklore and Traditional Magic

1. *Aradia, or the Gospel of the Witches* by Charles G. Leland
   - A seminal text in witchcraft folklore, this book details the legends, spells, and beliefs of Italian witches, blending history with magical instruction.

2. *Earth Power: Techniques of Natural Magic* by Scott Cunningham
   - Focused on the use of natural elements like stones, weather, and the Earth itself, this book offers practical guidance for nature-based magic.

3. *The Long-Lost Friend: A 19th-Century American Grimoire* by John George Hohman
   - A historical text of Pennsylvania Dutch folk magic, this book contains spells, charms, and remedies rooted in European and American traditions.

4. *Sacred Plant Medicine: The Wisdom in Native American Herbalism* by Stephen Harrod Buhner
   - This book explores the spiritual and medicinal uses of plants in Native American traditions, emphasizing their connection to healing and magic.

V. Astrological and Celestial Magic

1. *Astrology for the Soul* by Jan Spiller
   - A detailed exploration of lunar nodes and their influence on personal growth and spiritual development.
2. *The Secret Language of Astrology: The Illustrated Key to Unlocking the Secrets of the Stars* by Roy Gillett
   - A visually rich introduction to astrology, covering planetary influences, star charts, and celestial events.
3. *Lunar Abundance: Cultivating Joy, Peace, and Purpose Using the Phases of the Moon* by Ezzie Spencer
   - A practical guide to working with lunar cycles to manifest intentions and create balance in life.
4. *Planetary Magic: Invoking and Directing the Powers of the Planets* by Denning and Phillips
   - This book provides a detailed framework for incorporating planetary energies into magical rituals.

VI. Specific to Rose Hall and Caribbean Magic

1. *Jamaican Folk Medicine: A Source of Healing* by Arvilla Payne-Jackson and Mervyn Alleyne
    ◦ This book explores the healing traditions of Jamaica, including herbal remedies, spiritual practices, and cultural beliefs.
2. *Obeah: A Sorcery of the Caribbean* by Ioan Myrddin Lewis
    ◦ An in-depth study of Obeah, a magical and spiritual tradition originating in the Caribbean, with comparisons to Voodoo and other practices.
3. *The White Witch of Rose Hall* by H. G. de Lisser
    ◦ A fictionalized account of Annie Palmer, the infamous White Witch of Rose Hall, offering a glimpse into the legend's enduring mystique.

Using This Reading List

- **Beginner Practitioners**: Start with foundational texts like Starhawk's *The Spiral Dance* or Scott Cunningham's works to build a strong knowledge base.
- **Intermediate Practitioners**: Explore more specialized topics such as Voodoo (*Haitian Vodou Handbook*) or advanced spellcraft (*The Sorcerer's Secrets*).
- **Advanced Practitioners**: Dive into ceremonial magic, planetary influences, or the esoteric teachings in texts like *High Magick* or *Modern Magick*.

This collection of texts spans multiple traditions, providing resources for all levels of practice. Whether seeking historical context, practical guidance, or inspiration, these books will expand your under-standing of magic's many dimensions.

Appendix E: Supplies and Sources: Where to Find Magical Tools, Herbs, and Ingredients

The success of your magical practice often depends on the quality and energy of the tools, herbs, and ingredients you use. This appendix provides a detailed guide to sourcing reliable, ethically obtained magical supplies, whether you prefer to shop locally, online, or craft items yourself.

I. Essential Supplies
Magical Tools

1. **Athames and Ritual Knives**: Used for directing energy and symbolic cutting in rituals.
    - **Sources**: Look for handcrafted knives from blacksmiths or pagan specialty stores online (e.g., Etsy, Sacred Mists Shop).
    - **DIY Option**: Repurpose a knife with a wooden or bone handle; cleanse and consecrate it for magical use.
2. **Candles**: Used for spellwork, each color corresponding to a specific intention.
    - **Sources**: Purchase unscented candles from metaphysical shops or craft stores. Beeswax or soy candles are preferable for eco-friendly magic.
    - **Recommended Brands**: Tamed Wild, Crystal Journey Candles.
3. **Wands**: Tools for directing energy, often crafted from wood or crystals.
    - **Sources**: Local artisan markets or online crystal shops. Etsy has many custom wand makers.

- **DIY Option**: Create a wand from a fallen branch (e.g., oak, willow, or ash) and embellish it with crystals, paint, or symbols.

4. **Scrying Mirrors and Bowls**: Reflective surfaces used for divination.
   - **Sources**: Find black mirrors at occult stores or create one by painting the back of a glass plate with black paint.
   - **DIY Option**: Use a dark-colored bowl filled with water for scrying.

5. **Incense and Burners**: Used for purification, meditation, and setting the ritual atmosphere.
   - **Sources**: Purchase incense from metaphysical shops or Indian and Middle Eastern markets. Look for natural, hand-rolled options (e.g., Satya, Shoyeido).
   - **DIY Option**: Make your own loose incense by blending dried herbs, resins, and essential oils.

Herbs and Plants

1. **Common Herbs (e.g., Rosemary, Basil, Mint):**
   - **Sources**: Grocery stores, farmers' markets, or grow them at home for the freshest energy.
   - **Recommended Brands**: Mountain Rose Herbs, Starwest Botanicals.
2. **Rare or Exotic Herbs (e.g., Mugwort, Wormwood, Mandrake):**
   - **Sources**: Specialty metaphysical shops or herbal suppliers. Ensure they're ethically sourced.
   - **Recommended Shops**: Alchemy Works, The Witch's Herbarium.
3. **Fresh vs. Dried**: Fresh herbs carry stronger life force energy, while dried herbs are more convenient and long-lasting.

Crystals and Stones

1. **Common Crystals (e.g., Clear Quartz, Amethyst, Rose Quartz):**
   - **Sources**: Crystal shops, holistic wellness stores, and online retailers.
   - **Recommended Brands**: Energy Muse, Healing Crystals.
2. **Rare Crystals (e.g., Moldavite, Shungite):**
   - **Sources**: Reputable online sellers with certification of authenticity.
   - **Trusted Retailers**: The Crystal Council, Mystic Elements.
3. **Ethical Sourcing**: Ensure your crystals are ethically mined. Look for sellers who support fair-trade practices.

Oils and Potions

1. **Essential Oils**:
   - **Sources**: Buy from reputable brands specializing in therapeutic-grade oils (e.g., Young Living, Plant Therapy, or Eden's Garden).
   - **DIY Option**: Infuse oils like olive or almond with dried herbs to create your own anointing oils.
2. **Potion Ingredients**:
   - **Sources**: Many ingredients like honey, vinegar, and alcohol can be found at grocery stores. For rare items, check apothecaries or metaphysical suppliers.
   - **Recommended Brands**: Moonlit Herbals, Art of the Root.

Candles, Salt, and Common Ritual Items

1. **Salt (e.g., Sea Salt, Himalayan Salt)**:
   - **Sources**: Grocery stores, health food stores, or metaphysical shops.
   - **Uses**: Cleansing, protection, and grounding rituals.
2. **Charcoal Disks**: For burning loose incense or herbs.
   - **Sources**: Spiritual supply stores or online marketplaces like Amazon.
   - **Recommended Brands**: Three Kings Charcoal, Swift-Lite.
3. **Glass Jars and Bottles**: For storing herbs, oils, and potions.
   - **Sources**: Craft stores (e.g., Michael's, Hobby Lobby) or online retailers.
   - **Eco-Friendly Option**: Reuse and cleanse jars from home (e.g., empty spice jars or candle jars).

II. Online Retailers for Magical Supplies

1. **Mountain Rose Herbs**
   - Website: www.mountainroseherbs.com
   - Specializes in: Organic herbs, teas, essential oils, and tinctures.
2. **Tamed Wild**
   - Website: www.tamedwild.com
   - Specializes in: Monthly ritual boxes, candles, herbs, and magical tools.
3. **The Green Man Store**
   - Website: www.thegreenmanstore.com
   - Specializes in: Herbal remedies, magical tools, and workshops.
4. **Alchemy Works**
   - Website: www.alchemy-works.com
   - Specializes in: Rare and exotic herbs, resins, and oils.
5. **The Witch's Moon**
   - Website: www.thewitchesmoon.com
   - Specializes in: Curated ritual boxes, spell kits, and handcrafted items.
6. **Mystic Convergence Metaphysical Shop**
   - Website: www.mysticconvergence.com
   - Specializes in: Crystals, tarot decks, and ritual supplies.

III. Local Resources and Community

1. **Farmers' Markets**: A great source for fresh herbs, honey, and natural ingredients.
2. **Occult Shops**: Many cities have local occult or metaphysical stores offering supplies, workshops, and personalized advice.
3. **Botanicas**: Stores specializing in spiritual items and often catering to Voodoo, Santería, or similar traditions.
4. **Gardening Stores**: Perfect for purchasing seeds or tools to grow your own magical herbs.

IV. Ethical and Eco-Friendly Practices

1. **Sustainable Sourcing**: Ensure herbs and crystals are harvested responsibly to avoid overharvesting or exploitation.
2. **Support Local**: Whenever possible, buy from local artisans, farmers, or markets to reduce your environmental impact.
3. **Reuse and Recycle**: Repurpose containers, jars, and tools to minimize waste.

V. Crafting Your Own Tools

1. **Herb Gardening**: Grow plants like rosemary, basil, and lavender at home to have fresh, energetically aligned ingredients.
2. **DIY Incense**: Combine dried herbs and resins to create custom incense blends for specific rituals.
3. **Homemade Anointing Oils**: Infuse carrier oils with herbs, flowers, or essential oils to create personalized blends.

Conclusion

Sourcing high-quality magical tools and ingredients is an integral part of your practice. Whether you prefer crafting your own supplies, supporting local businesses, or purchasing from trusted online retailers, this guide ensures you have access to the materials needed for effective and ethical spellcraft. Let your tools be an extension of your intention, and approach every acquisition with mindfulness and gratitude.

Appendix F: Index of Spells

This appendix organizes all the spells featured in *The White Witch of Rose Hall's Spellbook* by type and intention, providing a quick-reference guide for practitioners. Whether you seek love, protection, prosperity, or spiritual insight, this index allows you to locate the right spell for your needs with ease.

I. Protection Spells

Spells designed to shield you, your loved ones, or your home from harm, negativity, or spiritual interference.

- **Nightmares Banishing Spell** (Chapter 16)
    - Intention: To prevent bad dreams and ensure restful sleep.
    - Tools: Black candle, salt, obsidian.
- **Protection Oil Spell** (Chapter 19)
    - Intention: To create a shield against illness or negative energy.
    - Tools: Olive oil, dried basil, rosemary, eucalyptus.
- **Salt Circle Spell** (Chapter 15)
    - Intention: To create a sacred, protected space.
    - Tools: Sea salt, white candle, bowl of water.
- **Spirit Warding Amulet** (Chapter 11)
    - Intention: To guard against restless or malevolent spirits.
    - Tools: Black cord, obsidian, rosemary, salt.

II. Love and Relationship Spells

Spells to attract love, strengthen bonds, or enhance passion.

- **Erzulie Freda Ritual for Love and Beauty** (Chapter 15)
    - Intention: To invite love and enhance personal charm.
    - Tools: Pink or red candle, rose petals, perfume.
- **Passion Flame Spell** (Chapter 15)
    - Intention: To reignite intimacy and deepen romantic connection.
    - Tools: Red candle, cinnamon stick, photograph.
- **Bond-Strengthening Charm** (Chapter 15)
    - Intention: To foster trust and emotional connection.
    - Tools: Blue cloth, dried lavender, rose petals, quartz crystal.
- **Marriage Blessing Ritual** (Chapter 15)
    - Intention: To strengthen marital harmony and long-term commitment.
    - Tools: White candles, white string, bowl of honey.

III. Prosperity and Abundance Spells

Spells to attract wealth, success, and opportunities.

- **Money Magnet Spell** (Chapter 14)
    - Intention: To draw financial opportunities and wealth.
    - Tools: Green candle, magnet, dollar bill, basil, cinnamon.
- **Golden Opportunity Spell** (Chapter 14)
    - Intention: To open doors to success and career advancement.
    - Tools: Gold candle, allspice, citrine or tiger's eye.
- **Abundance Jar Spell** (Chapter 14)
    - Intention: To maintain a steady flow of prosperity.
    - Tools: Small jar, coins, dollar bill, dried mint, basil, bay leaves.
- **Prosperity Coin Charm** (Chapter 14)
    - Intention: To enhance financial growth.
    - Tools: Shiny coin, dried mint, green pouch.

IV. Healing and Cleansing Spells
Spells to restore physical, emotional, or spiritual balance.

- **Herbal Healing Ritual for Physical Ailments** (Chapter 19)
    - Intention: To support recovery and physical well-being.
    - Tools: White candle, chamomile, rosemary, thyme, warm water.
- **Spiritual Cleansing with Florida Water** (Chapter 19)
    - Intention: To remove emotional burdens and purify the aura.
    - Tools: Florida Water, bowl of water, white cloth.
- **Emotional Healing with Rose and Lavender** (Chapter 19)
    - Intention: To release pain and foster self-love.
    - Tools: Pink candle, dried rose petals, lavender, rose quartz.
- **Healing Ward Spell** (Chapter 19)
    - Intention: To create a barrier against illness.
    - Tools: Black tourmaline, bowl of salt, green or white candle.

V. Divination and Psychic Spells

Spells to enhance intuition, connect with spirits, or reveal hidden truths.

- **Third Eye Activation Spell** (Chapter 12)
  - Intention: To enhance clairvoyance and spiritual perception.
  - Tools: Purple candle, amethyst crystal, lavender oil.
- **Dream Clarity Spell** (Chapter 12)
  - Intention: To receive vivid, meaningful dreams.
  - Tools: Mugwort tea, moonstone, notebook.
- **Tarot Spell for Decision-Making** (Chapter 12)
  - Intention: To gain clarity on a complex decision.
  - Tools: Tarot deck, white candle, bowl of water.
- **Scrying Mirror Ritual for Vision** (Chapter 12)
  - Intention: To access visions and spiritual insights.
  - Tools: Black mirror or bowl of water, silver candle, mugwort incense.

VI. Shadow and Light Spells

Spells to balance opposing forces and harmonize inner energies.

- **Shadow and Light Harmony Spell** (Chapter 20)
    - Intention: To integrate shadow and light energies within oneself.
    - Tools: White and black candles, quartz crystal, parchment.
- **Lunar Equilibrium Spell** (Chapter 20)
    - Intention: To balance energies using lunar influence.
    - Tools: Silver candle, dark gray candle, bowl of water, silver coin.
- **Shadow Integration Ritual** (Chapter 20)
    - Intention: To confront and embrace inner darkness.
    - Tools: Black mirror, black candle, obsidian.
- **Light Mastery Ritual** (Chapter 20)
    - Intention: To amplify positive energy and inner light.
    - Tools: White or gold candle, bowl of water, sunstone.

VII. Binding and Banishing Spells

Spells to restrict harmful influences or remove negativity.

- **Cord Binding Spell** (Chapter 13)
    - ◦ Intention: To neutralize the actions of a harmful person.
    - ◦ Tools: Black cord, folded paper, black candle.
- **Salt and Smoke Banishing Ritual** (Chapter 13)
    - ◦ Intention: To cleanse a space of negative energy.
    - ◦ Tools: Sage bundle, bowl of salt, bell or chime.
- **Circle of Light Banishing Ritual** (Chapter 13)
    - ◦ Intention: To purify and protect a space with light energy.
    - ◦ Tools: White candle, clear quartz, bowl of water.
- **Reversal Spell with a Black Candle** (Chapter 18)
    - ◦ Intention: To send a hex or curse back to its source.
    - ◦ Tools: Black candle, mirror, salt.

VIII. Dream and Sleep Spells

Spells to ensure restful sleep, lucid dreaming, or astral travel.

- **Lucid Dreaming Pillow Sachet** (Chapter 16)
    - ◦ Intention: To enhance awareness and control in dreams.
    - ◦ Tools: Mugwort, lavender, clear quartz, small pouch.
- **Astral Travel Talisman** (Chapter 16)
    - ◦ Intention: To support safe and guided astral projection.
    - ◦ Tools: Silver charm, blue ribbon, sandalwood oil.
- **Moonlight Dream Prophecy Ritual** (Chapter 16)
    - ◦ Intention: To harness dreams for prophetic insights.
    - ◦ Tools: Silver candle, moonstone, bowl of water.

IX. Forbidden and Dire Spells

Spells reserved for advanced practitioners and extreme situations.

- **The Spell of Invincible Will** (Chapter 21)
    - Intention: To cultivate unbreakable resolve.
    - Tools: Gold and black candles, obsidian, drop of blood (or alternative).
- **The Curse of Absolute Justice** (Chapter 21)
    - Intention: To ensure karmic retribution for harm caused.
    - Tools: Black candle, broken glass, photograph.
- **The Thorn Hex** (Chapter 21)
    - Intention: To restrain harmful actions without causing severe damage.
    - Tools: Thorny branch, black candle, folded paper.

Conclusion

This index serves as a quick reference for finding spells to suit your needs. Use it to locate the most effective practices for your goals, ensuring you align your intentions with the appropriate magical tools and energies. Let this be your guide as you explore the powerful magic within *The White Witch of Rose Hall's Spellbook*.

<u>**Message from the Author:**</u>

I hope you enjoyed this book, I love astrology and knew there was not a book such as this out on the shelf. I love metaphysical items as well. Please check out my other books:

-Life of Government Benefits

-My life of Hell

-My life with Hydrocephalus

-Red Sky

-World Domination:Woman's rule

-World Domination:Woman's Rule 2: The War

-Life and Banishment of Apophis: book 1

-The Kidney Friendly Diet

-The Ultimate Hemp Cookbook

-Creating a Dispensary(legally)

-Cleanliness throughout life: the importance of showering from childhood to adulthood.

-Strong Roots: The Risks of Overcoddling children

-Hemp Horoscopes: Cosmic Insights and Earthly Healing

- Celestial Hemp Navigating the Zodiac: Through the Green Cosmos

-Astrological Hemp: Aligning The Stars with Earth's Ancient Herb

-The Astrological Guide to Hemp: Stars, Signs, and Sacred Leaves

-Green Growth: Innovative Marketing Strategies for your Hemp Products and Dispensary

-Cosmic Cannabis

-Astrological Munchies

-Henry The Hemp

-Zodiacal Roots: The Astrological Soul Of Hemp

- **Green Constellations: Intersection of Hemp and Zodiac**

-Hemp in The Houses: An astrological Adventure Through The Cannabis Galaxy

-Galactic Ganja Guide

Heavenly Hemp

Zodiac Leaves

Doctor Who Astrology

Cannastrology

Stellar Satvias and Cosmic Indicas

Celestial Cannabis: A Zodiac Journey

AstroHerbology: The Sky and The Soil: Volume 1

AstroHerbology:Celestial Cannabis:Volume 2

Cosmic Cannabis Cultivation

The Starry Guide to Herbal Harmony: Volume 1

The Starry Guide to Herbal Harmony: Cannabis Universe: Volume
2

Yugioh Astrology: Astrological Guide to Deck, Duels and more

Nightmare Mansion: Echoes of The Abyss

Nightmare Mansion 2: Legacy of Shadows

Nightmare Mansion 3: Shadows of the Forgotten

Nightmare Mansion 4: Echoes of the Damned

The Life and Banishment of Apophis: Book 2

Nightmare Mansion: Halls of Despair

Healing with Herb: Cannabis and Hydrocephalus

Planetary Pot: Aligning with Astrological Herbs: Volume 1

Fast Track to Freedom: 30 Days to Financial Independence Using AI, Assets, and Agile Hustles

Cosmic Hemp Pathways

How to Become Financially Free in 30 Days: 10,000 Paths to Prosperity

Zodiacal Herbage: Astrological Insights: Volume 1

Nightmare Mansion: Whispers in the Walls

The Daleks Invade Atlantis

Henry the hemp and Hydrocephalus

10X The Kidney Friendly Diet

Cannabis Universe: Adult coloring book

Hemp Astrology: The Healing Power of the Stars

Zodiacal Herbage: Astrological Insights: Cannabis Universe: Volume 2

<u>Planetary Pot: Aligning with Astrological Herbs: Cannabis Universes: Volume 2</u>

Doctor Who Meets the Replicators and SG-1: The Ultimate Battle for Survival

Nightmare Mansion: Curse of the Blood Moon

<u>The Celestial Stoner: A Guide to the Zodiac</u>

Cosmic Pleasures: Sex Toy Astrology for Every Sign

Hydrocephalus Astrology: Navigating the Stars and Healing Waters

Lapis and the Mischievous Chocolate Bar

Celestial Positions: Sexual Astrology for Every Sign

Apophis's Shadow Work Journal: : A Journey of Self-Discovery and Healing

Kinky Cosmos: Sexual Kink Astrology for Every Sign

Digital Cosmos: The Astrological Digimon Compendium

Stellar Seeds: The Cosmic Guide to Growing with Astrology

Apophis's Daily Gratitude Journal

Cat Astrology: Feline Mysteries of the Cosmos

The Cosmic Kama Sutra: An Astrological Guide to Sexual Positions

Unleash Your Potential: A Guided Journal Powered by AI Insights

Whispers of the Enchanted Grove

Cosmic Pleasures: An Astrological Guide to Sexual Kinks

369, 12 Manifestation Journal

Whisper of the nocturne journal(blank journal for writing or drawing)

The Boogey Book

Locked In Reflection: A Chastity Journey Through Locktober

Generating Wealth Quickly:

How to Generate $100,000 in 24 Hours

Star Magic: Harness the Power of the Universe

The Flatulence Chronicles: A Fart Journal for Self-Discovery

The Doctor and The Death Moth

Seize the Day: A Personal Seizure Tracking Journal

The Ultimate Boogeyman Safari: A Journey into the Boogie World and Beyond

Whispers of Samhain: 1,000 Spells of Love, Luck, and Lunar Magic: Samhain Spell Book

Apophis's guides:

Witch's Spellbook Crafting Guide for Halloween

<u>Frost & Flame: The Enchanted Yule Grimoire of 1000 Winter Spells</u>

<u>The Ultimate Boogey Goo Guide & Spooky Activities for Halloween Fun</u>

Harmony of the Scales: A Libra's Spellcraft for Balance and Beauty

The Enchanted Advent: 36 Days of Christmas Wonders

Nightmare Mansion: The Labyrinth of Screams

Harvest of Enchantment: 1,000 Spells of Gratitude, Love, and Fortune for Thanksgiving

The Boogey Chronicles: A Journal of Nightly Encounters and Shadowy Secrets

The 12 Days of Financial Freedom: A Step-by-Step Christmas Countdown to Transform Your Finances

Sigil of the Eternal Spiral Blank Journal

A Christmas Feast: Timeless Recipes for Every Meal

Holiday Stress-Free Solutions: A Survival Guide to Thriving During the Festive Season

Yu-Gi-Oh! Holiday Gifting Mastery: The Ultimate Guide for Fans and Newcomers Alike

Holiday Harmony: A Hydrocephalus Survival Guide for the Festive Season

Celestial Craft: The Witch's Almanac for 2025 – A Cosmic Guide to Manifestations, Moons, and Mystical Events

Doctor Who: The Toymaker's Winter Wonderland

Tulsa King Unveiled: A Thrilling Guide to Stallone's Mafia Masterpiece

Pendulum Craft: A Complete Guide to Crafting and Using Personalized Divination Tools

Nightmare Mansion: Santa's Eternal Eve

Starlight Noel: A Cosmic Journey through Christmas Mysteries

The Dark Architect: Unlocking the Blueprint of Existence

Surviving the Embrace: The Ultimate Guide to Encounters with The Hugging Molly

The Enchanted Codex: Secrets of the Craft for Witches, Wiccans, and Pagans

Harvest of Gratitude: A Complete Thanksgiving Guide

Yuletide Essentials: A Complete Guide to an Authentic and Magical Christmas

Celestial Smokes: A Cosmic Guide to Cigars and Astrology

Living in Balance: A Comprehensive Survival Guide to Thriving with Diabetes Insipidus

Cosmic Symbiosis: The Venom Zodiac Chronicles

The Cursed Paw of Ambition

Cosmic Symbiosis: The Astrological Venom Journal

Celestial Wonders Unfold: A Stargazer's Guide to the Cosmos (2024-2029)

The Ultimate Black Friday Prepper's Guide: Mastering Shopping Strategies and Savings

Cosmic Sales: The Astrological Guide to Black Friday Shopping
Legends of the Corn Mother and Other Harvest Myths
Whispers of the Harvest: The Corn Mother's Journal
The Evergreen Spellbook
The Doctor Meets the Boogeyman
If you want solar for your home go here: https://www.harborsolar.live/apophisenterprises/

Get Some Tarot cards: https://www.makeplayingcards.com/sell/apophis-occult-shop

Get some shirts: https://www.bonfire.com/store/apophis-shirt-emporium/

<u>Instagrams:</u>
@apophis_enterprises,
@apophisbookemporium,
@apophisscardshop
Twitter: @apophisenterpr1
Tiktok:@apophisenterprise
Youtube: @sg1fan23477, @FiresideRetreatKingdom
Hive: @sg1fan23477
CheeLee: @SG1fan23477

Podcast: Apophis Chat Zone: https://open.spotify.com/show/ 5zXbrCLEV2xzCp8ybrfHsk?si=fb4d4fdbdce44dec

Newsletter: https://apophiss-newsletter-27c897.beehiiv.com/